AND JUSTICE FOR ALL

THE QUEST FOR CONCORD

VOLUME I

The Problem Defined

New York Times Bestselling Author

ORRIN WOODWARD

EDITED BY CHRIS BRADY | FOREWORD BY DR. GREG J. BRANNON

OBSTACLES PRESS

First Edition, May 2014
10 9 8 7 6 5 4 3 2 1

Published by:
Obstaclés Press
4072 Market Place Dr.
Flint, MI 48507

orrinwoodward.com

ISBN 978-0-9913474-9-0

Cover design and layout by Norm Williams, nwa-inc.com

Printed in the United States of America

To my children: Jordan, Christina, Lance, and Jeremy. May the concepts presented in this book be the catalyst for a rebirth of liberty in Western civilization in your lifetimes.

On Justice

Justice is the crowning glory of the virtues.

Justice consists in doing no injury to men…

*Justice is the set and constant purpose
which gives every man his due.*

*The foundations of justice are that no one should suffer
wrong; then, that the public good be promoted.*

…justice must be observed even to the lowest.

Justice does not descend from its pinnacle.

*Justice extorts no reward, no kind of price;
she is sought…for her own sake.*

Extreme justice is extreme injustice.

*If our lives are endangered by plots or violence…any and
every method of protecting ourselves is morally right.*

—Cicero

A state, or civitas is made harmonious by agreement among dissimilar elements, brought about by a fair and reasonable blending together of the upper, middle, and lower classes, just as if they were musical tones. What the musicians call harmony in song is concord in a State [civitate concordia], the strongest and best bond of permanent union in any commonwealth; and such concord can never be brought about without the aid of justice.

—Cicero

CONTENTS

FOREWORD

Thomas Jefferson said, "If a nation expects to be ignorant and free, in a state of civilization, it expects what never was and never will be."[1] He was saying that we must lay the foundation to build a truly free civilization to capture the best and to limit the worst of humans, society, and government that will lead to justice for all. George Washington supposedly said, "Government is not reason; it is not eloquent; it is force. Like fire, it is a dangerous servant and a fearful master."[2] We are seeing that fire spread in our government today and feeling its dangerous effects as it burns through our God-given rights.

This has led me to believe that we must ask ourselves these two questions: (1) Who is sovereign (because the source of sovereignty is the source of all power)? and (2) What is the legitimate role of government? Both questions are answered in the second paragraph of the Declaration of Independence, which starts: "We hold these truths to be self-evident, that all men are created equal, that they are endowed by their Creator with certain unalienable Rights, that among these are Life, Liberty and the pursuit of Happiness."[3] This charter doesn't declare to England why we should be free, but to the world why the individual will be free. Our country is founded on Judeo-Christian principles that lead to individual freedom.

Who is sovereign? We are endowed by our Creator and given inalienable rights; among these are life, liberty, and the pursuit of happiness. This clear statement declares that the Sovereign of the universe made us with certain inalienable rights. It is evident that our inalienable rights came *before* government. We are His expression on earth; therefore, we are sovereign. Life begins at the moment of conception and continues until our natural death. Liberty is the ability to fully express the God-given potential that He gave us during that lifetime. And pursuit of happiness is a summation or fulfillment of our infinite individual rights.

What is the legitimate role of government? The very next sentence in the Declaration of Independence explains this. It says, "That to secure these rights, Governments are instituted among Men, delivering their just powers from the consent of the governed."[4] The people give their consent for their individual rights to be protected. Any government that oversteps those rights is now illegitimate. Jefferson listed twenty-eight things that he calls tyranny because they overstep their bounds. A law can only be a constitutional law if it is based on God's natural law. Otherwise, it is the rule of man, which always seeks for a few to dominate the many. Under the natural rule of law, people are born free, made in the Creator's image. A law must protect the individual from the collective.

In this phenomenal book, Orrin Woodward articulates these principles in a logical process. He defines the Six Duties of Society that set up the structure of civilization, where the individual can blossom and society is at its best. He also defines the Five Laws of Decline, which are showing in today's society, and lays down some practical examples. George Santayana said, "Those who cannot remember the past are condemned to repeat it."[5] Patrick Henry said, "I have but one lamp by which my feet are guided, and that is the lamp of experience. I know of no way of judging the future, but by the past."[6] Through historical examples and analysis, Orrin clearly shows the traps we must avoid.

It is our generation's turn to step up. Benjamin Franklin stated on September 17, 1787, "We have a republic if you can keep it."[7] Concerning that republic, he challenged his generation. He sat in Philadelphia for five months while George Washington was presiding over the Constitutional Convention. Franklin would gaze behind the chair where Washington sat. Behind that chair was an engraving of half of a sun, and he asked his generation, "Is that a sunrise or a sunset?" That generation's answer was clear: a sunrise. This generation must ask the same question!

In the pages to follow, we can see the roadmap to attain our goal of the laws of the free if, and only if, we are truly the home of the brave!

James Madison said, "Knowledge will forever govern ignorance; and a people who mean to be their own governors must arm themselves with the power which knowledge gives."[8] Knowledge is our most powerful weapon that we must hold onto firmly so that we may eradicate any intrusion into our God-given inalienable rights!

—Dr. Gregory J. Brannon
Romans 12:9

INTRODUCTION

For over 2,500 years, Western civilization has been on a quest for concord (peace and justice) within society. Despite the best efforts of countless ancient, medieval, and modern societies, this quest remains unconsummated. The ability of society to create the proper balance of force and freedom has proven to be more elusive than one might imagine. The few civilizations in history that did achieve concord were unable to maintain it. The challenge revolves around just how much force free society needs in order to maintain justice for all. On one hand, when too much force is applied, freedom is lost as society falls into coercion by all-powerful rulers. On the other hand, when too much freedom is given, justice is lost as society falls into the chaos of competing factions fighting for control.

The freedom and force movements within society oscillate like a pendulum's trajectory between chaos and coercion, with concord in the middle. I created the Power Pendulum construct in an attempt to visually demonstrate the freedom/force ratio within society.

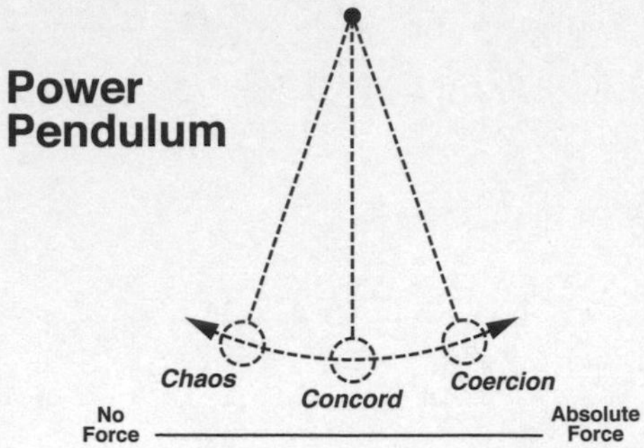

Considering a pendulum, it can be seen that as force increases in society, the pendulum moves toward coercion. Conversely, as freedom increases in society, the pendulum moves toward chaos. Of course, the goal of every just society is to rest the Power Pendulum in concord—wherein enough force is provided to ensure justice for all, and other than that, society's members enjoy the freedom to design lives of their own choosing.

Unfortunately, placing the Power Pendulum in this position of concord has proven problematic. Although several societies in history have enjoyed concord for a season, none have achieved it permanently. Moreover, in today's quick fix political culture, few leaders seek long-term systemic solutions to society's woes, preferring an endless string of bandages instead of the required surgery. Thus, to solve the quest for concord, we must first identify the underlying causes of the Power Pendulum's movements. By evaluating how the best societies achieved concord even temporarily and learning what eventually caused their drift into chaos or coercion, we can piece together the underlying contributors to societal failure.

In essence, modern societies cannot improve upon past attempts until they learn the appropriate lessons from them. The Power Pendulum is a tool to aid in this process. Once the causes of the Power Pendulum's shifts are properly identified, Western civilization can truly get on with the business of fulfilling its 2,500-year quest for concord.

Citizen, Society, and State

Every civilization can be broken down into three main components: citizen, society, and state. The Power Pendulum measures the force/freedom levels of these three components in relation to each other within a civilization.

Historically, the earliest human civilizations were marked with excessive coercion as the state practically absorbed society and its members into its force sphere. For example, the Egyptian kings were all-powerful rulers whose personal whims created the law of the land. These arbitrary laws were followed because they were backed by the king's control of the state's military force. Anyone foolish enough to resist the king's commands suffered death or imprisonment. Liberty, in a word, was rarely experienced in such coercive societies.

Not surprisingly, the kings exploited the people for the benefit of themselves and their cronies. The kings and their favored few lived luxuriously, while the rest were plundered into poverty. More disconcerting, the masses had few avenues for advancement since the key positions were reserved for the kings' supporters. Hence, with little opportunity to improve their lives, the masses lived a Hobbesian life that was "nasty, brutish, and short."[1]

The Greeks, in contrast, through a series of political innovations, designed society upon the revolutionary concept of liberty. Although ancient Greece had kings like the rest of its contemporary societies, the Greek kings did not have absolute power. Instead, the Greeks insisted that everyone, including the king, be under the rule of law. The king was responsible for ensuring justice by enforcing the law rather than creating laws for his personal benefit. This innovation changed the ancient world, since Greek citizens, as a result, enjoyed justice protected by the rule of law being applied to all. Instead of the traditional *rex lex* ("king is law"), the Greeks were the first to make it *lex rex* ("law is king").

Furthermore, because the Greek city-states were independent, any innovation that improved one city-state's liberty or productivity was quickly applied by other city-states. Indeed, the Greeks' love of competition in sports, art, economics, and politics led to levels of innovation and liberty not seen again until the Renaissance. For the first time in history, commoners with no aristocratic blood had a ladder to climb to the top of society based strictly upon their talents and work ethic rather than their bloodline. The rule of law provided a level of justice for all citizens never before seen in the ancient world. Directly because of this, the Greeks far surpassed the larger, oppressive neighboring empires in creativity and productivity.

The rule of law providing justice for all was a revolutionary concept and is a principal reason the Greeks are recognized as the progenitors of Western civilization. Nevertheless, the remarkable growth from this new societal framework did not endure. The Greeks quickly moved from concord into chaos, and liberty was snuffed out as the city-states battled each other for power. Still, the Greeks opened to the world the possibility of liberty and order within society, thus initiating Western civilization's quest for concord over 2,500 years ago.

Citizens

Although the Greeks loved liberty, it was centered more upon the city-state than the individual. Not until Judeo-Christian influences mixed with the Greco-Roman views did the center of liberty shift from society to the individual. The pagan worldview believed society was eternal and humans were temporary, but the Christian worldview reversed this by teaching that people were eternal and society was temporary. In effect, it was the confluence of these two streams of thought upon the conceptual domains of law and liberty, the state versus society, and God in relation to humankind that created Western civilization's worldview. Because God had provided humanity with life, liberty, and property, people judged societies based upon their ability to protect these God-given rights.

The story of liberty and justice progressed from only kings experiencing these privileges (in the early empires such as Egypt) to society-centered liberty and justice (in Greco-Roman times), finally culminating with all of society's members enjoying liberty and justice (in Western civilization). Edmund Opitz expressed the importance of humans in Western society when he wrote:

> Man's destiny is not simply to be a creature of society or the state; this is the beehive or anthill conception of life. Each man has an individual destiny which enables him to emerge out of society and propels him beyond it; he has a soul, for whose proper ordering he is responsible to his Creator.[2]

People, in other words, are not ants to be sacrificed indiscriminately by the whim of all-powerful rulers or all-consuming societies; rather, Western civilization views (or is supposed to view) people as eternal agents of God, who, through liberty and justice, apply their specific gifts and talents for His glory. And when they do so, families, societies, and nations prosper.

Above all, Western thought emphasizes that each individual liberty enjoyed is supported by a corresponding responsibility. Humans have been freed from the ancient anthill existence, where they merely did the bidding of the king, and now may enjoy the liberty and responsibility to develop their gifts and talents in the service of their God, family, and society. Although the emphasis on the individual's rights and responsibilities originated in Judeo-Christian teachings, it is now mainstream in Western civilization's thought.

For instance, Murray Rothbard, an agnostic economist and historian noted, "The glory of the human race is the uniqueness of each individual, the fact that every person, though similar in many ways to others, possesses a completely individuated personality of his own."[3] Each person has particular gifts and talents and a responsibility to develop them. As the Bible states in Luke 12:48 (NASB), "From everyone who has been given much, much will be required." Liberty is an inheritance provided to us by the Providence of God and the sacrifice of our predecessors. Our responsibility is to cherish, develop, and pass on this gift in better shape than we received it.

Lord Acton, the distinguished English historian, summarized humanity's duty as follows: "The doctrine of self-reliance and self-denial, which is the foundation of political economy, was written as legibly in the New Testament as in the *Wealth of Nations*."[4] This is the great breakthrough of Western civilization. No longer are people mere objects to be used for the state's or society's ends. Instead, society and government are God's institutions created to help people fulfill their calling in the world below before facing His judgment in the world above.

To be sure, liberty has its limits, since a person does not have the liberty to deny others their liberty. The goal of a free society is to provide liberty and justice for all members to grow and benefit from their gifts, talents, and purpose. John Locke identified justice in society with the protection of a person's inalienable rights to life, liberty, and estate (property). Locke, because he was a Christian, taught that these rights are inalienable, since humans are made by God, have an eternal soul, and are born with them before entering society. They cannot be justly denied to anyone except those who have violated another person's inalienable rights. In addition, because people join society to enjoy the benefits of increased life, liberty, and property, any coercion to deny inalienable rights is unjust and counter to the specific reason for joining society in the first place.

To conclude then, human beings have inalienable rights that cannot be denied them by either society or the state. When these rights are secured, the Power Pendulum moves into concord as people enjoy their inalienable rights and fulfill their responsibilities through working cooperatively with others.

Society

Society is the natural result of individuals discovering they can survive and thrive better by working together than they can apart. Individuals are drawn into communities for the social, economic, and political benefits. Opitz explains, "Scarcity in the human realm makes society necessary. Society is at the very least a labor-saving device, and therefore it is needed by creatures who must economize by conserving scarce goods."[5] Furthermore, since people are "political animals," as Aristotle wrote, they seek society for the social enjoyment along with political protection. As a result, people have social, economic, and political incentives to form societies. Economist Wilhelm Röpke said, "Man can wholly fulfill his nature only by freely becoming part of a community and having a sense of solidarity with it. Otherwise he leads a miserable existence and he knows it."[6]

Society, simply stated then, is humanity's natural solution to social, economic, and political needs. In the economic sphere, society increases the number of occupations from which a person can choose to achieve economic self-sufficiency. Moreover, as society expands, the workforce naturally increases in specialization, thereby improving the skills and technological know-how of its members. This increased specialization leads to greater productivity and a practically unlimited range of career choices for its members. Rothbard explains:

> For, as an economy grows[,] the range of choice open to the producer and to the consumer proceeds to multiply greatly. Furthermore, only a society with a standard of living considerably higher than subsistence can afford to devote much of its resources to improving knowledge and to developing a myriad of goods and services above the level of brute subsistence.[7]

For that reason, when society enjoys liberty and justice, people can plan, do, check, and adjust (what I call the PDCA process) appropriately to achieve their goals and dreams and in the process lift society as a whole. Needless to say, every society that has protected people's inalienable rights has also prospered.

Albert Jay Nock coined two terms—Social Power and State Power—to describe how power accumulates within society. Social Power grows when free people enjoying liberty and justice order their lives by persuading others to cooperate with them in a win–win fashion. Regrettably, however, not everyone within society seeks win–win scenarios. If the possibility exists for the strong to oppress the weak, one can rest assured that someone will choose this win–lose antisocial path instead. This is when those seeking advancement by means other than merit hijack government power. Then, driven by such individuals, State Power starts to grow as government gets stronger and stronger and infringes upon the freedoms of society's people.

Governments and States

Antisocial behavior arises as people seek to satisfy their wants with as little effort as possible. Disgracefully, most will even go so far as to oppress others to achieve this objective whenever the opportunity is available. Put another way, humans have a natural propensity to try to reap where others have sown in order to satisfy their wants through "something for nothing" (SFN).

Historically, just as a strong person exploits a weaker one, a strong society exploits a weaker society. Hence, a just society must develop a systematic method to check this antisocial behavior of people and society. If not, exploitation occurs as the strong parasitically plunder the production of the weak.

Government is society's solution enacted to limit exploitation and injustice. James Madison described the reason government is necessary when he wrote, "If men were angels, there would be no need for government."[8] But since humans aren't part of the angel family, society must form a government with a delegated monopoly of force to protect its members from potential internal and external plunderers. Government, as a result, is the only entity within society founded upon force rather than freedom. While the rest of society secures cooperation through persuasion, the government, in contrast, secures justice through violence. In most cases, just the threat of violence is enough to deter potential plunderers, but when force is needed (as in the defense of one's country), it is important for the government to be given sufficient force to fulfill its delegated purpose.

Unfortunately, however, a government's delegated monopoly of force is difficult to maintain within its designated boundaries. This leads to an accumulation of power within the once-limited government. This is the paradox of government's monopoly-of-force power. On the one hand, government must have the force to properly fulfill its function of defense, but on the other hand, government rulers are not angelic beings either. Bertrand de Jouvenel pinpointed this precise challenge when he wrote, "Power is neither angel nor brute, but, like man himself, a composite creature, uniting in itself two contradictory natures."[9]

Since society assigned government the task of checking the contradictory nature within its members, an answer must be provided to the question: Who is assigned to check the contradictory nature within government's members? If the concern about the strong exploiting the weak led to society creating government with a monopoly of force, certainly society must also create a method to ensure that the monopoly of force is held in check. Otherwise, the very government assigned to protect the people against oppression becomes the biggest oppressor of those people.

Nock described the beginning of tyranny as occurring when government oversteps it boundaries in order to grow its State Power at the expense of Social Power:

> It is unfortunately none too well understood that, just as the State has no money of its own, so it has no power of its own. All the power it has is what society gives it, plus what it confiscates from time to time on one pretext or another; there is no other source from which State power

> can be drawn. Therefore every assumption of State power, whether by gift or seizure, leaves society with so much less power; there is never, nor can be, any strengthening of State power without a corresponding and roughly equivalent depletion of social power.[10]

Consequently, society must create a government with sufficient force to defend against injustice but at the same time check government with another power capable of resisting government efforts to step outside its delegated boundaries. As we shall see, the reason no society has yet successfully fulfilled the quest for concord is because not one has simultaneously delegated appropriate force to government to keep society out of chaos while also restraining government's growth enough to keep society out of coercion. Although numerous methods have been attempted to restrain government's monopoly of force, regrettably, none of them have proven to be effective in the long term at limiting the growth of government's power. That is the reason the Power Pendulum has historically oscillated between chaos and coercion, with only intermittent periods of concord.

Since human beings hate chaos even more than they hate coercion, the pendulum has spent more time in coercion than it has in chaos. Although coercion is not the desired condition, if society cannot enjoy concord, then it would rather endure coercion with order than chaos with disorder. For the most part, chaos occurs when government is too weak to maintain peace within society. The resulting power vacuum quickly swings the Power Pendulum in the direction of chaos as different groups battle for sovereignty over society. Coercion, in contrast, occurs when government applies too much force within society in the effort to overcome chaos.

Because government is designed specifically to use force, it behaves like a construction worker who only uses a hammer and, as a result, views everything as a nail. Government is society's monopoly-of-force hammer used to nail internal and external plunderers who attempt to commit injustice. Since the one tool delegated to government is the force hammer, it should be applied exclusively when it is the only tool capable of accomplishing the job. In essence, State Power should never enter any area where the force hammer is not needed. By restraining State Power to its proper function, Social Power can fulfill the rest of society's functions.

Unfortunately, few seem to understand this crucial point. Hence, government's force hammer smashes into areas of society in which it is not needed or wanted, and productive members of society end up nailed by the undiscriminating governmental force. As government expands into new areas of action, it increases its State Power and feeds parasitically on Social Power, just as Nock warned. Therefore, to rest the Power Pendulum in concord, society must build Social Power through liberty and persuasion while limiting State Power to the necessary role of checking potential aggressors from committing unjust win–lose antisocial acts. Then, and only then, will society ensure liberty and provide justice for all.

The quest for concord will not be fulfilled until society designs a government that can be maintained within its delegated limits. This is a worthy quest because every society that has experienced concord (peace and prosperity by providing justice for all) for even a generation has far surpassed the creativity, technology, and productivity levels of its rival societies. Curiously, however, despite the indisputable evidence in favor of concord and justice for all, few societies ever strive to achieve justice for all their members. Even among those few who do, none have determined how to maintain this justice against the growth of State Power over time. Why?

The key in answering this was provided by sociologist Franz Oppenheimer's distinction between the two methods of wealth creation: the "economic means" and the "political means." In his magnum opus *The State*, he wrote:

> There are two fundamentally opposed means whereby man, requiring sustenance, is impelled to obtain the necessary means for satisfying his desires. These are work and robbery, one's own labor and the forcible appropriation of the labor of others.
>
> Robbery! Forcible appropriation! These words convey to us ideas of crime and the penitentiary, since we are the contemporaries of a developed civilization, specifically based on the inviolability of property. And this tang is not lost when we are convinced that land and sea robbery is the primitive relation of life, just as the warriors' trade—which also for a long time is only organized mass robbery—constitutes the most respected of occupations. Both because of this, and also on account of the need of having, in the further development of this study, terse, clear, sharply opposing terms for these very important contrasts, I propose in the following discussion to call one's own labor and the equivalent exchange of one's own labor for the labor of others, the "economic means" for the satisfaction of needs, while the unrequited appropriation of the labor of others will be called the "political means."[11]

When people utilize the "economic means" to create wealth, Social Power (the dispersed power of society's members) increases, and society prospers. Conversely, when people utilize the "political means" to expropriate wealth, State Power (the centralized power of the state) increases, and society withers. Therefore, the main reason society seeks to limit government is to limit the growth in State Power and thus the growth in the unjust "political means" of wealth expropriation. When State Power is checked from growing at society's expense, this frees Social Power to thrive by utilizing the just "economic means" of wealth creation.

Oppenheimer, in essence, identified two separate paths for riches: the just method of using persuasion and the unjust method of using force. Since the "economic means" utilizes persuasion, it thrives under liberty and justice within society, and Social Power is maximized. In contrast, since the "political means" needs coercion, it thrives under force and injustice within society, and State Power is maximized. The method society applies to generate wealth (either the just "economic means" or the unjust "political means") ultimately determines whether societal members' inalienable rights are protected.

There is an underlying systemic cause behind the "rise-and-fall" cycle of every society. The process causing society's "rise" occurs when members utilize "economic means" to increase Social Power. In this book, we will call this the Six Duties of Society (SDS). Conversely, the process causing society's "fall" occurs when members utilize "political means" to increase State Power. We will call this the Five Laws of Decline (FLD).

In effect, when the SDS are satisfied, societies rise. When the FLD are unleashed, societies fall. In summation, the rise-and-fall cycle follows naturally from the rise and fall of Social Power and

State Power, which are related to the method of wealth generation ("economic means" or "political means") society employs.

When one applies these concepts to history, it becomes apparent that the FLD and SDS models can explain the rise-and-fall cycle of every historical society. And very quickly, we also see why all previous societies have failed in their quest for concord. Furthermore, and most important, the SDS and FLD systemic models provide the key to fulfilling the quest for concord today.

The key breakthrough is the realization that the struggle between the rise-and-fall cycle within society parallels the struggle between the "angel and brute" nature within humanity. Depending upon which part of human nature is rewarded or punished according to the method of wealth generation used (the "economic means" or the "political means"), society will either grow or decline. Put another way, it is the inherent dual nature within humans affecting how they treat others—through either cooperation or compulsion—that predictably leads to the rise-and-fall cycle in society. Hence, Oppenheimer's two methods employed to gain wealth are directly related to the duality of human nature.

The first method, the "economic means," employs justice, liberty, and concord. The second method, the "political means," employs injustice, force, and coercion. The first builds Social Power, while the second builds State Power. Crucially, since human beings refuse to produce beyond the level of justice they receive, the greater the injustice within society, the less wealth is created. Therefore, the rise-and-fall cycle of society results from the path chosen by its members for building wealth. Since human beings respond to justice and injustice predictably, the "economic means" within society (employing Social Power methods of persuasion and cooperation) achieves much greater productivity than does the "political means" (employing State Power methods of antisocial force and fraud).

Not surprisingly, because government uses its monopoly of force to perform its role as society's protector against internal and external injustice, it likewise becomes a tempting prize for exploiters seeking to use this force to achieve "political means" of wealth expropriation. When exploiters gain control of a government, they quickly pass laws to benefit themselves and their supporters. If anyone in society objects, the exploiters use the monopoly of force to ensure compliance with the unjust laws.

Absurdly, the exploiters in this scenario have turned the government, which was responsible for ensuring justice for all, into the enforcement agency providing benefits to only some. Indeed, modern states have countless unjust "political means" laws designed to benefit the few at the expense of the many. Nonetheless, humanity always resists oppression, to some degree and in some way. Therefore, if society has no legal recourse available, the members will simply reduce their efforts until the injustice stops or they are producing at bare subsistence levels. Either way, the injustices will be reduced since, paraphrasing Margaret Thatcher, the state will run out of other people's money to steal.[12] Simply put, the more injustice reigns, the less production results. Hence, the less wealth there is for the exploiters to confiscate by "political means."

Compulsion, in effect, may force the human body to obey, but it can never command the heart. For human beings do not produce results in captivity as do draft animals. Instead, they steadily lower their performance as injustice grows. This simple but profound fact reveals why progressive increases in the level of justice produce progressively higher levels of creativity and productivity within society. Author Warren T. Brookes captures how the duality within both human nature and the methods for creating wealth has led to a division within the science of economics as well:

> One view, defined by Adam Smith and Jean-Baptiste Say, is that wealth is primarily metaphysical, the results of ideas, imagination, innovation, and individual creativity, and is therefore, relatively speaking, unlimited, susceptible to great growth and development. . . . After all, if wealth truly is metaphysical, the result more of mind than matter, the "wealth of nations" has to be seen as the direct result of the creative activity of individuals and the degree to which that activity is either liberated or restricted by governmental, trade, or societal structures and strictures. . . . The other, espoused by Thomas Malthus and Karl Marx, contends that wealth is essentially and primarily physical, and therefore ultimately finite. The modern presentation of this view argues that since usable energy is steadily diminishing into entropy, all wealth is really cost to be shared more equitably. . . . If one believes that wealth is primarily a function of material resources, and is therefore limited (or declining), it is only natural that one would see the role of economic policy as the just and collective conservation, distribution, and redistribution of these limited resources until the end is reached.[13]

Smith and Say believe wealth is metaphysical, and since ideas are unlimited, society should employ the "economic means" of wealth creation to raise the tide of humanity and its societal ships. In contrast, Malthus and Marx believe wealth is physical, and since resources are limited, society should employ the "political means" of wealth expropriation to direct the tide equitably between societal ships. This divergence in economic thought relates back to the divergence in methods to create wealth, which tracks back to the divergence within humans themselves.

One of the key objectives of this book is to educate leaders in the systematic interaction between these two opposing forces within society. For only when this is understood can we achieve long-lasting concord within society. Toward that end, three questions must be answered in order to achieve enduring concord within society:

1. What areas of society prosper best under liberty and persuasion?
2. What is the proper role of government within society to ensure justice for all?
3. How does society check government's monopoly of force from expanding into areas where it doesn't belong?

Although Western civilization has never achieved enduring concord, a systematic understanding of the SDS and FLD provides the breakthrough needed for its long-term success.

CHAPTER ONE

STATE AND SOCIAL POWERS

The word *society* derives from the Latin word *socius,* which is defined as a companion. People, as Aristotle once wrote, are "political animals" and naturally seek companionship with other human beings. Moreover, since every person is unique, one of society's greatest benefits is the economic improvements possible when people focus in fields that magnify their gifts and talents. Humans, in other words, leave their independent pre-society existence (state of nature) to seek interdependent life within society for social and economic benefits. Above all, however, the main reason they leave the state of nature to join society is to more securely protect their inalienable rights of life, liberty, and property. John Locke wrote:

> Why will he give up this empire, and subject himself to the dominion and control of any other power? To which it is obvious to answer, that though in the state of nature he hath such a right, yet the enjoyment of it is very uncertain, and constantly exposed to the invasion of

> others: for all being kings as much as he, every man his equal, and the greater part no strict observers of equity and justice, the enjoyment of the property he has in this state is very unsafe, very unsecure. This makes him willing to quit a condition, which, however free, is full of fears and continual dangers: and it is not without reason, that he seeks out, and is willing to join in society with others, who are already united, or have a mind to unite, for the mutual *preservation* of their lives, liberties and estates, which I call by the general name, *property*.[1]

Overall, societal liberty grows as individual members practice self-restraint to build Social Power. Therefore, the paradoxical conclusion is that a voluntary decrease in personal freedoms of society's members results in the cooperative increase of societal liberty. Educator Felix Morley explains:

> Regardless of the social institution we stop to consider—whether it be the family as the oldest known cooperative unit, or an association of atomic scientists as a modern manifestation—we see similar evidences of self-imposed restraint. Husband and wife put definite limits on their individual freedom, in order to promote certain objectives, such as the rearing of children, which they have in common. And the atomic scientists in congress assembled are making comparable individual sacrifices for their particular common end. So it seems to be the nature of human association, whether voluntary or involuntary, to limit the condition of freedom for those whose association is something more than merely casual.[2]

The responsible self-restraint practiced by society's members is, in consequence, the key element in building Social Power to form a free and prosperous society. This self-restraint implies internal discipline by society's members rather than an external discipline imposed upon them. This is because achievers happily discipline themselves so as to accomplish their goals in interdependent communities. Thus, responsible members restrain personal freedoms to enlarge societal liberty.

For instance, imagine if car drivers demanded the freedom to drive on either side of the road at will. This act of driver freedom would quickly lead to chaos and a subsequent loss of liberty because no one would be safe on the roads. Curiously, the increase in driver freedom results in a decrease in societal liberty, since driving is only safe when people deny themselves a degree of personal freedom to follow the rules of the road. Indeed, if drivers refuse to practice self-restraint, society suffers a loss in liberty because no society can afford a police officer for every driver to force them to adhere to the rules of the road. Unfortunately, however, every time society's members seek freedom over self-restraint for the sake of society, it results in an increase in governmental external restraints (State Power) to fill the vacuum created by the lack of responsible internal restraints (Social Power), and liberty is lost.

Therefore, the part of human nature (angel or brute) that is rewarded depends upon whether society is founded upon freedom or force. For example, only in a freedom society can a person practice disciplined personal responsibility, since in a force society, a person practices obedience out of fear of punishment. A free society, in essence, allows its members to learn the difference between responsible actions for the good of all within the community and irresponsible actions that benefit themselves at the expense of others. As a result, free societies use leadership persuasion (Social Power), while unfree societies use coercive force (State Power). Indeed, only in free societies can real leaders, who practice persuasion to influence, develop. In contrast, coercive societies typically build bureaucracies that enforce member compliance through coercion.

Morley clarified how free societies teach responsibility without coercion to build Social Power when he wrote:

> That which is limited by continuous association is the indulgence of individual appetites, passions, and animal instincts—the carnal side of man. That which is expanded by continuous association is the perfection of individual skills, ambitions, and aspirations—the spiritual side of man. Thus, continuous voluntary association may and does limit the physical condition of freedom. But it does so to enlarge the moral endowment of liberty.[3]

In effect, societies grow when self-imposed individual restraints build Social Power rather than when external restraints build State Power.

Ever since pre-society people lived in what Locke termed the "state of nature," individuals have been responsible for protecting their personal right to life, liberty, and property themselves. In fact, Locke believed these three rights so essential to humankind that he described them as inalienable (that is, they cannot be taken away). Claude Frédéric Bastiat summarized Locke's inalienable rights when he wrote:

> Life, faculties, production—in other words, individuality, liberty, property—this is man. And in spite of the

> cunning of artful political leaders, these three gifts from God precede all human legislation and are superior to it. Life, liberty, and property do not exist because men have made laws. On the contrary, it was the fact that life, liberty, and property existed beforehand that caused men to make laws in the first place.[4]

Western civilization, by combining the best of Greco-Roman and Judeo-Christian worldviews, believed humans were made in the image of God and had the right and responsibility to protect their life, liberty, and property. Each of these three inalienable rights must be clearly understood to ensure they remain inalienable even after people enter society.

The first inalienable right states that all people have a right to live and that no one can take this right from them. Thus, if their life is threatened, they have a right to defend themselves against that threat. Indeed, the Judeo-Christian worldview teaches that only when people willfully violate another human being's right to life do they forfeit the right to their own.

The second inalienable right expresses people's liberty to pursue their specific interest without coercion from their neighbors, society, or government. In fact, liberty is only limited in that a person does not have the right to deprive another person of the same liberty. For instance, people are free not to read certain books or attend certain meetings, but they do not have the right to deny others the opportunity to read or attend, since this would limit the other people's liberty.

Finally, the third inalienable right—the right to own property—expands upon the preceding two, since both life and liberty are special types of ownership (of one's life and actions). Private property is essential to the uniqueness of

Western civilization because it allows the members of society a zone of liberty protected from individual, organizational, or governmental interference. People have a right to own property, and what is theirs cannot be taken from them by any outside entity. In this way, they can work, accumulate, and use their wealth however they choose. In effect, without private property protection, people in society are no different than ants in an anthill—replaceable units of little value. There simply is no substitute for private property, and it is one of the keys to the near-miraculous levels of productivity and liberty experienced in the Western societal framework when compared to all others.

Since these three rights are inalienable to humans and precede their entrance into political society, it logically follows that political society did not grant these rights to its members, nor can it violate them without committing an act of injustice. Accordingly, any government that deprives people of their inalienable rights has negated its delegated duty and has become illegitimate. Indeed, just as Locke taught, in such circumstances, the people have the natural right to withdraw consent from the tyrannical regime. People, in other words, do not join society to give up or lose their rights and responsibilities for their life, liberty, and property but rather so they can protect and maximize them. Stated more simply, a good society does not deny humanity's inalienable rights but rather enhances them.

The state of nature for humankind, interestingly, is similar to the status of sovereign nations in the world. Just as people protect their rights from the aggression of other people, so must each nation protect its members from the aggression of other nations. In both cases, since no higher authority is available to help adjudicate a dispute, the conflict between the parties must be settled through either reason or aggression. Unfortunately, the exploitive nature inherent within humans usually leads to both stronger individuals and stronger nations plundering their weaker counterparts. Although persuasion is effective in every other area of society, it is ineffective in checking humanity's exploitive nature.

Consequently, society, in an effort to systematically ensure justice for all, forms a government and delegates to it a monopoly of force to use, when needed, to defend its members' life, liberty, and property. Instead of each member having to produce with one hand while defending with the other, government embodies a form of division of labor instituted to protect society, thereby allowing the members to focus on production. It follows that since government protects the rights of everyone within the society, each citizen benefiting from that protection ought to pay his or her fair share of the cost. When members receive the benefits of government's justice *without* paying the bill, they are called free-riders.

Douglass Cecil North and Robert Paul Thomas elaborated on how government's monopoly of force overcomes the free-rider dilemma:

> Threatened by marauders, the producers of goods and services responded by investing in military defense. But the building of a fortress and the enlistment of soldiers immediately raised the specter of the free-rider. Since the fortress and troops could hardly protect some villagers without protecting all, it was to each man's advantage to let his neighbor do the paying if contributions were on a voluntary basis. Thus, defense, as a classic case of a public good, involves the problem of excluding third parties from the benefits. The most effective solution

> was, and continues to be, the forming of governmental authorities and taxing of all beneficiaries. Justice and the enforcement of property rights are simply another example of a public good publicly funded.[5]

Society solves the free-rider challenge through delegating to government a monopoly-of-force hammer. Government then utilizes this hammer to specialize in internal and external justice by defending the inalienable rights of society's members. This is government's only legitimate function: protection of its members' inalienable rights to life, liberty, and property. The rest of society's members, as a result, can focus on production in their specific fields, since government provides the defense function for everyone.

As mentioned before, when government protects its members' inalienable rights with justice for all, society thrives. In contrast, when government, through tyranny over the members' inalienable rights, becomes unjust, society dives. Indeed, government is supposed to check injustices, not create them. Regrettably, if government does not address injustices, the members' inalienable rights are damaged, and the door is opened for further injustices to occur.

There are three main avenues of injustice within society.

The first is the strong members of society oppressing the weak. Since people seek to satisfy their wants with the least amount of effort, if plunder is unchecked within society, the strong will plunder the weak, and injustice will reign.

The second type of societal injustice occurs when the government uses its force hammer outside its delegated and limited sphere of defense. Although society thrives under persuasion and only needs government's force hammer to check potential exploitation, when this hammer enters other areas of society, the government itself becomes an agent of injustice as it pounds people in areas where persuasion is just. Not surprisingly, as government intervention grows, so does State Power at the expense of Social Power. Government's force hammer damages society anytime it is used in areas that it doesn't understand and where it doesn't belong or help.

The third type of injustice occurs in society when it is invaded and defeated by a stronger nation seeking plunder. The victors promptly increase State Power to systematically plunder the defeated society. The vanquished society, however, still has methods to resist the systematic plunder of the conquerors. As the oppressive state plunders the life, liberty, and property of the conquered society's members, they respond in a predictable fashion. Even though they have been defeated militarily, they have not been defeated metaphysically. When injustice abounds within a society, the people's creativity and productivity respond accordingly. Thus, by simply reducing their productivity to the bare minimum necessary to survive, they rob the victors of the expected systematic plunder.

If anything above the sustenance level will just be plundered by the state, why would anyone produce any more than the bare minimum? Evidently, the state believes that when it maximizes oppression, it also maximizes plunder. But this simply isn't so. Society's members merely reduce their productivity as the state increases its tyranny. In fact, if the state does not relax its oppression, the death of the parasitic state and its societal host is assured. This is a common theme for all historically oppressive societies. Nevertheless, the state exploiters seem incapable of learning from history.

Why do the state exploiters destroy the societies they plunder? The answer, again, is rooted in human nature. Although human beings may have limited needs, they also have unlimited wants. As a result, when plunder is possible, the exploiters cannot seem to restrain their desire for just a little more.

As a matter of fact, Oppenheimer's research concluded that most states, instead of being formed by the consent of the governed, were, in reality, imposed upon society by conquerors. The foundation of most states, contrary to what many people believe, isn't in contracts between equal parties but rather in dictates from the victors to the defeated. Indeed, a study of any period of history reveals that nearly every time a wealthy society is weaker than another one, the stronger invades the weaker to reap where it hasn't sown. Of course, the subsequent state created by the invaders is formed not for society's benefit but for systematic plunder. Still, as discussed above, the conquered society refuses to produce under oppression like it did when its members enjoyed their inalienable rights.

Wise conquerors learn to limit the level of exploitation in order to reduce societal resistance to their rule. This ongoing bargain between State Power and Social Power permits a ruler to achieve the necessary consent of the governed to rule without rebellion. In other words, a wise exploiter restrains the state from plundering too much by preserving a basic degree of inalienable rights for society's members. This course of action secures the exploiter's rule and plunder for the long term. The conquering state, ironically, secures a level of justice in society, not due to the love of its subjects (remember, it previously invaded the society) but rather to promote production in the societal host that will benefit the parasitic state. In a sense, the state lightens its oppression in order to enjoy rewards without revolution.

If the tenuous balance between State and Social Power relies upon the restraint of self-disciplined leaders, it will not last because sooner or later someone will not be similarly restrained. Once that someone initiates further oppression of society for more plunder, the vicious cycle is activated wherein increased tyranny leads to decreased production. As we've seen, such circumstances, unchecked, lead to society's failure.

The important point is that State Power, even when led by competent leaders, is concerned about Social Power only insofar as it helps increase the production of society for the state's benefit. The conquering state's role over the defeated society is similar to a shepherd's role over a flock: to protect an investment, not typically out of love but rather out of self-interest. The shepherd rarely slaughters the sheep but instead just shears them closely.

This same principle, however, also works in reverse. The equilibrium between State and Social Power reduces the tyranny in the most oppressive states but increases it in less oppressive ones. On the one hand, even the most oppressive states need the consent of the governed to rule. The rulers will provide the people certain rights and liberties to win legitimacy and consent from the people. On the other hand, every once-limited government in history eventually transformed into a powerful state. This process naturally occurs when the power-hungry rulers make every societal emergency a tool for transferring more Social Power into State Power. Regrettably, when the emergency subsides, the state seldom surrenders its new power gains back to society. Thus, State Power grows at Social Power's expense until one cannot detect a difference between states formed by conquerors and those formed by the consent of the governed.

Regardless of how the state was founded, both types end up granting just enough protection of inalienable rights to ensure the people's submission rather than rebellion—that is, until the wrong leader assumes power and the increased oppression leads to either chaotic rebellion or coercive submission. Human societies, as a result, are in a never-ending struggle between the forces seeking to optimize State Power and those seeking to optimize Social Power.

There is a condition wherein both State and Social Power can grow together. It occurs when a limited government, through performing its proper function (internal and external justice), builds Social Power, which then builds the tax revenue base and, thus, State Power. This is the path to societal concord wherein neither State Power nor Social Power grows at the other's expense. Instead, they work in tandem to achieve concord and growth.

The United States in the nineteenth century is an example of a society that achieved temporary concord as both State Power and Social Power increased. The rising tide, so to speak, lifted both ships. Typically, however, win–win thinking in the political arena is in short supply. In most cases, State and Social Power wage an endless war for dominance in which a win for one is paid for by a loss of the other. This is why the Power Pendulum's quest for concord has not been achieved in an enduring fashion in any society.

For instance, every government, regardless of its origins (limited consensual government or powerful conquering state), seeks to maximize State Power without rebellion. Consequently, although nineteenth-century American society was a bastion of Social Power with limited State Power, one that immigrants from around the world fled to in an effort to enjoy inalienable rights, the state of affairs reversed course considerably during the twentieth century. Indeed, State Power consumed Social Power at such a rate that today there isn't any real difference between American society and the European societies that most of the immigrants sought to escape. The temporary concord of nineteenth-century America was replaced by the twentieth century's coercion.

State Power grows through the consolidation of society's responsibilities into state responsibilities. Social Power, on the other hand, is not consolidated but is rather the dispersed power of society's members seeking to improve their lives. Social Power grows when government is limited to securing justice while leaving all other areas of society free to develop solutions to their challenges through persuasion instead of compulsion. Unfortunately, State Power has an unbeatable advantage in its win–lose struggle against society's Social Power because the state can apply coercion where society only has persuasion. Thus, whenever society delegates the monopoly of force for government's limited defense role, it must also restrain government from using this force to expand into other areas. The dismal track record of unchecked State Power is intervention with force into practically every area of society. In addition, every promise by the state to help society comes at the price of increased State Power and decreased Social Power. Bastiat outlined the proper limits of government when he wrote:

> Each of us has a natural right—from God—to defend his person, his liberty, and his property. . . . If every person has the right to defend—even by force—his person, his liberty, and his property, it then follows that a group of men have the right to organize and support a common force (government) to protect these rights constantly. Thus, the principle of collective right—its reason for existing, its lawfulness—is based on the individual right. And the common force that protects this collective right

> cannot logically have any other purpose or any other mission than that for which it acts as a substitute. Thus, since an individual cannot lawfully use force against the person, liberty, or property of another individual, then the common force (government) cannot legitimately be used to destroy the person, liberty, or property of individuals or groups. . . . This common force of government is to do only what individuals have a natural and lawful right to do—to protect persons, liberties, and properties; to maintain equal rights of each person; and to cause justice to reign over us all.[6]

To ensure justice for all, the state must be restrained to use the force delegated to it only for the protection of citizens' inalienable rights. Bastiat, again, described such a just government:

> If a nation were founded on this basis, it seems to me that order would prevail among the people, in thought as well as deed. It seems to me that such a nation would have the most simple, easy to accept, economic, just, non-oppressive, limited, and enduring government imaginable.[7]

Provide society with justice for all, and concord (Social Power and State Power growing together) results. Similarly, a society suffering from repeated injustices results in chaos or coercion. To date, there has not been one case of a limited government that has not eventually grown into a powerful state. The failure modes seem to repeat again and again—societal growth under liberty and limited government and eventual death under the tyranny of an all-controlling state. How many more rise-and-fall historical examples are necessary before society learns its lesson? Society must realize the symbiotic relationship between liberty and justice to grow Social Power and enact effective checks on government's growth to limit State Power. Once this relationship between freedom and force is understood, society can take the right steps to restrict the government's monopoly of force to its proper role.

Another notable difference between the state and the rest of society is how the state gains power and wealth. The state lives off the production of society. At its best, the state is a useful dependent, using up some of the Social Power of society in order to ensure justice; at its worst, it is a painful parasite, consuming Social Power to initiate injustices until society collapses. When government is limited to providing justice, its expenditures are more than offset by increased productivity in society. In other words, the cost associated with a limited government defending its members' inalienable rights is covered by the gains in production by the society enjoying justice for all.

Is it truly possible for society to check the state's monopoly-of-force power advantage? This is, in fact, the unsolved state/society riddle that when answered will make the quest for concord achievable. All attempts throughout history have followed the same path of failure.

The cycle reminds me of the story of a merchant at a bazaar. He notices a bump in one of his rugs, so he steps on the bump to flatten it out. The bump, though, merely reappears in another spot. This process continues six more times until an angry snake crawls out from underneath the rug. The incredulous merchant, despite his repeated attempts to solve the problem he saw (the bump), didn't see the "systemic" reason for the problem (an underlying snake). In a similar fashion, most leaders seek to step on political "bumps" rather than solve the underlying systemic problems that are causing them.

If we are to ever achieve concord, we have got to deploy a better method than did our rug merchant. To help us do so, we need to first comprehend what we'll call the Six Duties of Society (SDS). The SDS are a systematic framework depicting how society operates to increase Social Power and societal prosperity. Accordingly, the SDS are crucial for understanding why society has not fulfilled its 2,500-year quest for concord.

CHAPTER TWO

THE SIX DUTIES OF SOCIETY

The Six Duties of Society (SDS) are a systematic framework developed to explain how a society builds a healthy culture by encouraging its members, through physical and metaphysical rewards, to expand their productive capacities to build Social Power. The six duties are as follows:

Physical

1. Distribution
2. Division of Labor
3. Duplication of Members
4. Defense

Metaphysical

5. Distinction (on Performance)
6. Dreams (Vision and Goals)

All civilizations must satisfy the SDS, or they will not grow. These six duties are essential for Social Power and can be divided into two subcategories: physical and metaphysical. The first four duties are physical requirements, ensuring the satisfaction of the people's physical needs within society. The last two are, in reality, even more important, since they focus on the metaphysical underpinnings of society.

The metaphysical duties inspire most of the members to support the mission and the reward structures of society. Because the metaphysical foundations of Western civilization are Judeo-Christian, where each human being is viewed as the centerpiece of God's creation, society is built for people rather than people for society. Indeed, societies are created by God to help people fulfill their responsibilities of being fruitful, multiplying, and having dominion over the earth. In other words, since humans are eternal and society is temporary, society can lay no claims upon a person's inalienable rights without overturning the intended order through treating what is temporary (society) as more important than what is permanent (a human soul).

In contrast to the Judeo-Christian view, the earlier Greco-Roman metaphysical foundations viewed society as eternal and humans as temporary. Thus, the Greco-Roman model reversed the proper order, and people were treated as replaceable ants in an irreplaceable anthill. The ancient societies believed that anytime the city was threatened, the people's rights could be violated in order to save the city because the city's existence was above human rights. These false metaphysical foundations could not endure, and when they collapsed, so too did the society. This is because the people no longer believed in or sacrificed for the metaphysical duties that previously united them.

Distribution of Goods

The first duty for a society is to develop distribution methods to flow the goods and services of its members to customers. Since all people must produce in order to survive, when they discover they have more than necessary, they naturally barter away the excess for other items that are needed more. This is a win–win scenario, since each party benefits by receiving goods with a higher perceived marginal value than the goods bartered away. Matt Ridley observed:

> A successful transaction between two people—a sale and a purchase—should benefit both. If it benefits one and not the other, it is exploitation, and it does nothing to raise the standard of living. The history of human prosperity, as Robert Wright has argued, lies in the repeated discovery of non-zero-sum bargains that benefit both sides. . . . The perpetual innovation machine that drives the modern economy owes its existence not mainly to science (which is a beneficiary more than its benefactor); nor to money (which is not always a limiting factor); nor to patents (which often get in the way); nor to government (which is bad at innovation). It is not a top-down process at all. Instead, I am going to try now to persuade you that one word will suffice to explain this conundrum: exchange. It is the ever-increasing exchange of ideas that causes the ever-increasing rate of innovation in the modern world.[1]

Free trade in products and ideas is a series of win–win transactions for both sides. In effect, it is the peaceful method for neighbors to benefit from one another's creativity and production without degenerating into war and exploitation. The popular aphorism "If goods don't cross borders, armies will" explains why free trade is so essential for peace. Instead of countries seeking to exploit each other's production, it is better for both sides to seek win–win trades. Barter, however, although win–win, is an inefficient method of trading because each party must want the other's goods, and it is difficult to determine the proper exchange ratio between the items. Finally, both parties must physically trade the items in order to complete the transaction, even if it proves costly to do so. Although fair, bartering is an extremely inefficient system.

The country of Lydia solved this inefficiency during the reign of King Croesus, when merchants created the world's first known gold and silver coins. Suddenly, instead of having to swap physical products, a person could sell his product to another, even if the customer had no product the seller wanted in return. Then, at a later time, the seller could barter these coins for any desired products or services. Economist William Gouge describes the use of what we now call money:

> Some fancy that it is the authority of Government that gives money its value. But the true value of money, as measured by the amount of goods for which it will honestly exchange, cannot be affected by edicts of Princes or acts of Parliament. Monarchs and Ministers may alter the weight of coins, or lessen their purity; but they cannot make a coin containing an half of an ounce of pure silver, worth as much as a coin containing an ounce. The stamp of the State is a mere certificate of the weight and fineness of the piece. . . . Corn, cattle, iron, leather, cocoa, tobacco, and other commodities, have all, in point of fact, been used as money, in different ages and different countries;

but they have long ceased to be so used, by commercial nations, for reasons similar to those which have induced men to choose for their standard of length, some object less liable to variation than the foot of a Chancellor, or the fore arm of a King.

The high estimation in which the precious metals have been held, in nearly all ages and all regions, is evidence that they must possess something more than merely ideal value. Men chose gold and silver for the material for money, for reasons similar to those which induced them to choose wool, flax, silk, and cotton, for materials for clothing, and stone, brick, and timber, for materials for building. They found the precious metals had those specific qualities, which fitted them to be standards and measures of value, and to serve, when in the shape of coin, the purposes of a circulating medium. To this use they are admirably adapted:

1. Because they are divisible into extremely minute portions, and capable of re-union without any sensible loss of weight or value; so that the quantity may be easily apportioned to the value of the articles of purchase.
2. They have a sameness of quality all over the world . . . one grain of pure gold is exactly similar to another, whether it comes from the mines of Europe or of America, or from the sands of Africa. Time, weather, and damp, have no power to alter the quality: the relative weight of any specific portion, therefore, determines its relative quantity and value to every other portion; two

grains of gold are worth exactly twice as much as one.

3. Gold and silver, especially with the mixture of alloy that they admit of, are hard enough to resist very considerable friction, and are therefore fitted for rapid circulation.
4. Their rarity and consequent dearness are not so great, that the quantity of gold or of silver, equivalent to the generality of goods, is too minute for ordinary perception: nor, on the other hand, are they so abundant and cheap, as to make a large value amount to a great weight.
5. They are capable of receiving a stamp or impression, certifying the weight of the piece, and the degree of its purity.
6. They are liable to less variation than any other article, from changes in the relations of supply and demand, including the cost of production among the conditions of supply.

Where metallic money is exclusively used, the value of land, of labor, and of all commodities, great and small, can be determined with great accuracy. If, in such countries, the trade between different men is not always an interchange of equivalents, the fault is not in the instrument of valuation, but in those who use it. If the labor of a man, for a day, or for a year produces more than is necessary for his immediate support, he can by exchanging the surplus product for gold or silver, secure the means of supplying his wants in future days or years. Time will not corrupt his treasure or lessen its value. If he

> should not require it all for his personal wants, he may, at the end of fifty years, endow his children with a portion. The use of money renders it unnecessary for families to keep on hand a large stock of provisions and other necessaries, and thus saves them from the risk of loss from provisions spoiling, and from various accidents. . . .
>
> Without money, the division of labor could never be carried to any great extent, and the wealth of society would be small. Money, by promoting commerce, advances civilization.[2]

Money, accordingly, is one of the greatest inventions in the history of humanity because it improved the exchange and distribution of goods between people.

Division of Labor

The second duty of society, division of labor, is one of the key reasons why people seek communities: to specialize in areas aligned with their natural abilities. The people divide the steps of production into smaller steps to focus more on a specific task. This leads to increased learning curves and innovation through further specialization.

Economist George Reisman identified six major ways the division of labor increases the productivity of labor, enabling people to apply their minds, bodies, and environment more efficiently and effectively:

1. It increases the amount of knowledge used in production by a multiple that corresponds to the number of distinct specializations and sub-specializations of employment.

2. It makes it possible for geniuses to specialize in science, invention, and the organization and production of others.
3. It enables individuals at all levels of ability to concentrate on the kind of work for which they are best suited on the basis of differences in their intellectual and bodily endowments.
4. It enables the various regions of the world to concentrate on producing the crops and minerals for which they are best suited on the basis of differing conditions of climate and geology.
5. It increases the efficiency of the processes of learning and motion that are entailed in production.
6. It underlies the use of machinery in production.[3]

Indeed, nearly all nonexploitive advances in society have occurred by expanding the distribution and division-of-labor duties. Conversely, if the distribution duty falters, so too does the division-of-labor duty. This reduces societal wealth, as each person must invest more time meeting survival needs at the expense of specialization.

Ridley describes specialization as one of the keys to societal growth:

> The cumulative accretion of knowledge by specialists that allows us each to consume more and more different things by each producing fewer and fewer is, I submit, the central story of humanity. Innovation changes the world but only because it aids the elaboration of the division of labor and encourages the division of time. Forget wars, religions, famines and poems for the moment. This is

> history's greatest theme: the metastasis of exchange, specialization, and the invention they have called forth, the "creation" of time.[4]

Although I do not believe this is history's greatest theme, I do believe it is essential for societal prosperity—and certainly one of society's six duties.

Duplication of Members

The third duty of a prosperous society is duplication of members, which leads to an expanding population. Healthy societies prosper when the first two duties are satisfied, and the increasing population feeds the growth of both. Interestingly, a society must reproduce at about 2.1 live births per family just to maintain its population. Any less, and the population begins to decline. From a production standpoint, a declining population slows the growth of the first two duties. Usually, a decline in population indicates a decline in its members' metaphysical hope for the future.

Today, dismally, many of the world's countries have dipped below the 2.1 threshold. For instance, both Japan and Germany hover around 1.3 live births per family. This is nothing short of a national catastrophe as these once-proud nations are on the verge of disappearing if the current trend continues.

The duplication duty is a must for a society's health, especially when one considers that no society has prospered for more than a couple of generations with a declining population. In contrast, high birth rates work with the first two duties to advance society forward. In fact, North and Thomas argue that Western civilization is a direct result of improved property rights along with the growth of European populations:

> The predominant parameter shift which induced the institutional innovations that account for the rise of the Western World was population growth. . . . We submit, therefore, that the development and expansion of a market economy during the Middle Ages was a direct response to the opportunity to gain from the specialization and trade made feasible by population growth. The growth in towns facilitated local and regional exchanges, and the expansion of these markets made it profitable to specialize functions, to introduce new technologies, and to adjust the production processes to altered conditions. In sum, a growing population created the basis for trade; the resulting expansion of the market economy caused the medieval economy to react, if slowly, precisely in the manner Adam Smith would have predicted.[5]

When government ensures justice and liberty, the expanding population (duplication duty) also expands the market (distribution duty), specialization (division of labor duty), and consequently, the productive capacity of a society. For a healthy growing society, then, population growth is a positive and not a negative.

Defense

The fourth duty of a working society is the only one better performed by a force government than a free society, namely, to defend and protect the inalienable rights of each member by ensuring justice for all. In effect, when a society produces wealth, that wealth becomes an irresistible temptation for both internal and external exploitation if there is not a sufficient force to deter such exploitation. One of the inherent faults of humans is their desire to reap where they have not sown. If just laws are not created and enforced to check humanity's rapacious nature, people will surely exploit fellow humans.

Sociologist Paul Seabright described this sobering truth when he wrote, "Where there are no institutional restraints on such behavior, systematic killing of unrelated individuals is so common among human beings that, awful though it is, it cannot be described as exceptional, pathological or disturbed."[6] To be just, society must create laws to which everyone, including those in power, must conform. To that end, the rule of law was one of the biggest breakthroughs of Western civilization and created the environment in which order and liberty could thrive together. Bastiat explained the crucial role of the rule of law when he wrote:

> What, then, is law? It is the collective organization of the individual right to lawful defense. Each of us has a natural right—from God—to defend his person, his liberty, and his property. These are the three basic requirements of life, and the preservation of any one of them is completely dependent upon the preservation of the other two. For what are our faculties but the extension of our individuality? And what is property but an extension of our faculties? . . . Law is organized justice. . . . When justice is organized by law—that is, by force—this excludes the idea of using law (government) to organize any human activity whatsoever, whether it be labor, charity, agriculture, commerce, industry, education, art, or religion. The organizing by law of any one of these would inevitably destroy the essential organization—justice. For truly, how can we imagine force being used against the liberty of peaceful citizens

without it also being used against justice, and thus acting contrary to its proper purpose?[7]

Societal injustices follow one of two paths: external or internal exploitation. The first is the story of weaker nations losing their sovereignty to stronger neighbors who seek to exploit the wealth of the weaker. The second is the story of the state seeking to exploit society's wealth through violating its members' inalienable rights. Since the primary role of government is the protection of its citizens' inalienable rights, both of these outcomes are governmental failures.

Regardless of whether a government can successfully exploit a weaker nation for power, prestige, and plunder, it should not do so because exploitation is not its delegated role. Indeed, its delegated task is to defend society, not attack another one.

Although external injustices frequently occur, internal injustices are an even bigger issue. The paradox within government is how to provide an entity with enough force/power to defend society without permitting it to oppress society. What force/power within society, for example, is capable of commanding government to go only so far but no further? Since government's overwhelming force advantage can ignore speeches, constitutions, and even the people (short of revolution), what counterweight can society develop to check governmental expansion into spheres where it doesn't belong?

Part of the answer may be surprising: Make sure government is not too weak to be able to perform its delegated task of ensuring justice. For when government is not strong enough to resolve internal conflicts peacefully, chaos ensues in the form of a civil war for power. This internal disorder causes the ruin of both the physical and metaphysical duties, and society declines.

Therefore, internally, in its defense duty, society must provide government with sufficient force to protect the inalienable rights of its citizens. Externally, this is achieved through military might for defense against outside aggressors.

Free societies remain free when they limit the sphere of government to areas where force is the only option possible to ensure justice for all. Bastiat aptly described the purpose of government, justice, and the law:

> The harmlessness of the mission performed by law and lawful defense is self-evident; the usefulness is obvious; and the legitimacy cannot be disputed. As a friend of mine once remarked, this negative concept of law is so true that the statement, *the purpose of the law is to cause justice to reign*, is not a rigorously accurate statement. It ought to be stated that *the purpose of the law is to prevent injustice from reigning*. In fact, it is *injustice*, instead of justice, that has an existence of its own. Justice is achieved only when injustice is absent. But when the law, by means of its necessary agent, force, imposes upon men a regulation of labor, a method or a subject of education, a religious faith or creed—then the law is no longer negative; it acts positively upon people. It substitutes the will of the legislator for their own wills; the initiative of the legislator for their own initiatives. When this happens, the people no longer need to discuss, to compare, to plan ahead; the law does all this for them. Intelligence becomes a useless prop for the people; they cease to be men; they lose their personality, their liberty, their property. Try to imagine a regulation of labor imposed by force that is not a violation of liberty; a transfer of wealth imposed

by force that is not a violation of property. If you cannot reconcile these contradictions, then you must conclude that the law cannot organize labor and industry without organizing injustice.[8]

Distinction

The previous duties involved the physical aspects of society, but the last two cover the even more important metaphysical ideas that drive society forward. The fifth duty of society, the distinction duty, is the first metaphysical one. It ensures a healthy distinction in society for those willing to perform.

Distinction focuses on the attitudes, ideas, and rewards that allow society's members to be recognized as they climb the social ladder of success. Indeed, every society has distinctions, but if they are rewards for wrong behavior ("political means" rather than "economic means"), the human spirit is damaged. Society, in other words, must fulfill humanity's need for recognition and a higher purpose in order to maintain the members' hunger to grow and change. Moreover, distinction can influence people's behavior through freedom rather than force by simply recognizing those who follow societal norms and by shunning those who don't.

Distinctions naturally occur within families, schools, professions, and communities. In truth, distinction is inherent within every human organization because it is part of human nature to recognize both the similarities and differences between people. The key is to identify the healthy distinctions and reward them, since what is rewarded increases.

In general, a healthy society acknowledges distinctions when people advance in areas that propel society upward. People are promoted based upon performance similar to how salespeople are awarded cars, trips, and promotions when achieving quotas.

Nonetheless, not all societal distinctions are healthy. When distinction is based upon race, creed, color, or sex, society blocks certain members with talent from rising to deserved levels. Furthermore, nebulous or indistinct levels reduce productivity and increase politicizing as people attempt to move up without the performance to merit doing so. Distinctions, then, must be based upon performance, not on political maneuvering.

Volunteers who freely invest time into community forums such as the various "wikis," YouTube, Linux, etc., are driving what can now be called a "reputation economy." Their motivation for doing so is recognition and distinction among their peers. As author Jeff Howe explained:

> It's about cred, or, to give that a more theoretical cast, it's about the emerging reputation economy, where people work late into the night on one creative endeavor or another in the hope that their community—be it fellow designers, scientists, or computer hackers—acknowledge their contribution in the form of kudos and, just maybe, some measure of fame.[9]

Distinction, in effect, drives people beyond the normal effort they would expend for mere monetary rewards. Thus, when distinction is not possible for most people within a society, productivity levels predictably decrease. Whereas distinction incentivizes societal growth, its absence disincentivizes the same.

Although distinction may appear to be a minor point, in reality, it is vitally important. People are not like draft animals, which can work obediently so long as they are provided food, drink, and shelter. In contrast, human beings must believe their efforts will lead to increased distinctions and rewards (metaphysical progress), or they will mentally "check out." Hence, a properly working society must recognize progress through the distinction of its members.

The Communists, who boasted of equality for all, unintentionally demonstrated that people are not satisfied with invisibility. Communism has consistently failed because people suffer metaphysical famine when they are forced to live lives that feel meaningless. Although the Communist system claimed equality for everyone, it hypocritically still provided distinctions for its obedient party members. What was prohibited for the masses was preserved for the elite. Hence, the go-getters in society logically migrated to the state. This had the effect of increasing State Power while damaging Social Power even more. In the end, by attacking the SDS with force and eliminating any individualization whatsoever for ordinary people, communism disproved itself.

Dreams

The sixth and most important duty is providing a way for society's members to dream and achieve. When society protects its members' inalienable rights and allows people to dream, set goals, and make plans, the productivity of society is practically assured. Cream rises to the top. So society is propelled forward when liberty permits everyone to dream and when the proper distinctions are provided for achievement.

Simply stated, without dreams, people quickly lose hope for the future. It has been said that one can live without food for forty days; one can live without water for four days; one can live without air for four minutes; but no one can live without hope for even four seconds. This being true, it is not surprising that when dreams are missing from society, suicide rates increase, birth rates decrease, and productivity levels plummet. Dreams, in other words, are essential for societal health.

Society advances then when it frees individuals to advance. Those who are advancing in their distinctions and dreams improve society as much as they improve themselves. One of Stephen Covey's seven habits of success is to "begin with the end in mind." He describes this concept as follows:

> Habit 2 is based on imagination—the ability to envision in your mind what you cannot at present see with your eyes. It is based on the principle that all things are created twice. There is a mental (first) creation, and a physical (second) creation. The physical creation follows the mental, just as a building follows a blueprint. If you don't make a conscious effort to visualize who you are and what you want in life, then you empower other people and circumstances to shape you and your life by default. It's about connecting again with your own uniqueness and then defining the personal, moral, and ethical guidelines within which you can most happily express and fulfill yourself. Begin with the End in Mind means to begin each day, task, or project with a clear vision of your desired direction and destination, and then continue by flexing your proactive muscles to make things happen.[10]

The more society celebrates those who begin with the end in mind and attain results accordingly, the more it motivates others to achieve additional distinction for themselves. In contrast, if no dreams are possible in a society, a debilitating demoralization infects the soul of that nation. Ridley wrote:

> Inventors will not invent unless they can keep at least some of the proceeds of their inventions. After all, somebody will not invest time and effort in planting a crop in his field if he cannot expect to harvest it and keep the profit for himself—a fact Stalin, Mao, and Robert Mugabe learned the hard way.[11]

Rare is the individual, in other words, who will strive for great accomplishments without the ability to reap the commensurate rewards.

The breakup of the Eastern Bloc of Communist countries is not surprising when one realizes that there were few opportunities for dream accomplishment (outside of the elite members of the Communist Party). This is all in addition to the lack of distinctions we discussed in the previous section. With no hope of dream realization, people's production soon fell below subsistence levels, and the boastful behemoth called communism collapsed under its own weight. It was a remarkable and historic day when the Berlin Wall was finally torn down, but from an SDS perspective, it wasn't shocking. When a people are denied the metaphysical duties needed for society to survive, primary among them being the opportunity to pursue worthwhile dreams, the resulting collapse is inevitable.

The Six Duties of Society as a System

These six duties work together to satisfy people's needs within society, creating an increase in Social Power. By satisfying the SDS, society provides liberty and justice to its members and thereby enables them to dream, think, and produce in pursuit of their own felt purposes. In reality, if people were provided liberty and justice across the world, many of the challenges facing us today would be solved through the resultant human innovation.

Not coincidentally then, throughout history, the societies that have satisfied the SDS have enjoyed the most impressive wealth and productivity. Justice, in a word, is the key, for it ensures that human beings, who are made in the image of God, are treated with the dignity and respect that title deserves. Then, when justice is secure, the people apply the "economic means" of wealth creation, and Social Power greatly expands. Authors Wayne Grudem and Barry Asmus expressed the systemic benefits that liberty and justice bring into society when they wrote:

> Free trade is as close to a perpetual motion machine as any economic idea of man. Trade produces economic gains; economic gains produce higher incomes; higher incomes allow people to buy more goods and services, which leads to even more efficient production which leads to ever more trade. The ever-widening circle of wealth causes more division of labor, more specialization, more productivity, and more benefits from mutual exchange and trade. Nations and people get rich when they trade freely.[12]

Once government has secured justice for the people's inalienable rights, the SDS naturally expand society's markets and production. Adam Smith described the SDS back in 1776 when he wrote:

> The natural effort of every individual to better his own condition, when suffered to exert itself with freedom and security is so powerful a principle that it is alone, and without any assistance, not only capable of carrying on the society to wealth and prosperity, but of surmounting a hundred impertinent obstructions with which the folly of human laws too often encumbers its operations; though the effect of these obstructions is always more or less either to encroach upon its freedom, or to diminish its security.[13]

A prosperous society expands when a free interchange between people, products, and ideas thrives under the conditions of justice for all. As a society trades goods and services with its neighbors, capital increases for both parties. As traders deposit their increased capital into banks, entrepreneurs can then borrow money. These entrepreneurs, accordingly, invest in new products, processes, and tools of production. All this expands the division of labor and increases efficiency. Hence, increased efficiency leads to lower prices and better quality. This expands the marketplace even further. Finally, the expanded marketplace leads to further production improvements, and the SDS are abundantly satisfied.

Since a just society naturally solves challenges through Social Power, it follows that the SDS cannot be satisfied until government sufficiently performs its duty of defense. When that happens, Social Power thrives. In effect, once justice is assured for society's members, Social Power does the rest. Increased prosperity naturally leads to population growth as people from around the world flock to the just and prosperous society. In addition, as Social Power increases, the limited government grows its revenues to maintain justice for all. However, even though the expanding Social Power does lead to a corresponding increase in State Power, it is the Social Power that is driving society forward. As Social Power satisfies the physical duties, the metaphysical duties also thrive because members achieve the distinction duty and the dream duty within society.

Therefore, humanity must develop a method of government that can satisfy the defense duty without encroaching into the other duties. Only in such a way can the prosperous condition described above occur. When government provides protection of the inalienable rights of society's members, the justice-for-all condition grows the SDS, creating an ever-widening circle of systemic prosperity. Historian Johan Norberg described the results possible when society satisfies the SDS:

> The growth of world prosperity is not a "miracle" or any other of the mystifying terms we customarily apply to countries that have succeeded economically and socially. Schools are not built, nor are incomes generated, by sheer luck, like a bolt out of the blue. These things happen when people begin to think along new lines and work hard to bring their ideas to fruition. But people do that everywhere, and there is no reason why certain people in certain places during certain periods of history should be intrinsically smarter or more capable than others. What makes the difference is whether the environment permits and encourages ideas and work, or instead puts obstacles in their way. That depends on whether people are free to explore their way ahead, to own property, to invest for the long term, to conclude private agreements

and to trade with others. In short, it depends on whether countries have capitalism.[14]

Forming a governmental system that satisfies the SDS is the only way for Western society to fulfill its quest for concord. As Bastiat explained:

> When successful, we would not have to thank the state for our success. And conversely, when unsuccessful, we would no more think of blaming the state for our misfortune than would the farmers blame the state because of hail or frost. The state would be felt only by the invaluable blessings of safety provided by this concept of government.... Since all persons seek wellbeing and advancement, would not a condition of justice be sufficient to cause the greatest efforts toward progress and the greatest possible equality that is compatible with individual responsibility? Would not this be in accord with the concept of personal responsibility that God has willed in order that mankind may have the choice between vice and virtue and the resulting punishment and reward?[15]

Paradoxically, it is the overwhelming success of the SDS that leads to their ultimate failure. Satisfying the SDS produces a prosperous society, which awakens exploiters to plunderous opportunities. Expanding wealth stimulates exploiters like a red flag does a bull, and they behave predictably according to the Five Laws of Decline (FLD).

Simply stated, the SDS drive society's rise, and the unchecked FLD cause its fall. A fulfilled SDS originally created Western civilization's prosperity, but that was not enough. To complete the quest for concord and provide justice for all, society must not only build the SDS but—even more important—stop the FLD from subsequently destroying them. Indeed, when the FLD are not effectively checked, it is just a matter of time before wealth is plundered by the state faster than society can create it.

As a consequence, the history of Western civilization is filled with rise-and-fall stories where satisfying the SDS led to a society's rise and not checking the FLD caused its fall. The next couple of chapters will explain the Five Laws of Decline in detail so that, in understanding them, we can determine how to successfully check them from cancerously growing within society.

CHAPTER THREE

INTRODUCING THE FIVE LAWS OF DECLINE

Throughout history, human beings have been capable of astounding acts of both good and evil. In fact, oftentimes, the same person performs remarkably humane and then inhumane actions in the same lifetime. Interestingly, the Judeo-Christian worldview predicts this inconsistent behavior since it teaches that, although people are made in God's image, our rebellion caused an alienation from God. Thus, our self-centered will is capable of spectacular deeds of both good (reflective of God) and evil (reflective of our nature apart from God).

On the one hand, people work cooperatively in a spirit of win–win justice, and the SDS (and therefore society) prosper. On the other hand, humans are capable of foul injustice in their efforts to exploit fellow human beings. Indeed, the genocides, mass murders, and confiscatory wars throughout history have produced a genuinely depressing record of "man's inhumanity to man."

The Five Laws of Decline (FLD) form a system designed to categorize and describe the outworkings of the exploitive side of human nature and their contribution to the decline of society. Those who understand the FLD, recognize the destruction at work anywhere human beings associate.

Paradoxically, it is when the Six Duties of Society (SDS) cause society to prosper that the danger from the FLD is the greatest. For the increased wealth resulting from the healthy SDS is practically an irresistible temptation to the exploitive nature within humans. Indeed, the greater the wealth society produces by just "economic means," the more innovative exploiters become in attempting to plunder it by "political means."

I first introduced the Five Laws of Decline in my book *RESOLVED: 13 Resolutions for LIFE*[1] in order to demonstrate how organizational leadership declines. A few years later, Oliver DeMille and I coauthored a book entitled *LeaderShift*,[2] which also features the FLD as they are germane to explaining the political decline of America. In general, political decline results when the unchecked FLD cause society to split into two groups: those who produce wealth and those who plunder it.

James Madison explained why people, since they are not angels, need a government to ensure justice by restraining exploiters from plundering society. When government performs its delegated role of protecting inalienable rights, society's members will naturally gravitate to the "economic means" of wealth creation, and society will flourish as it satisfies the SDS. For example, just as pickpockets avoid practicing their craft around police officers, so too do all exploiters steer clear of plunder when a just government punishes injustice.

Although government justice is absolutely necessary for a thriving society, it is vital to remember that government, like society overall, also consists of less-than-angelic men and women. So while government is necessary to protect one person from exploiting another, it is also necessary to protect people in society from that very same government. In truth, since government is delegated the monopoly-of-force hammer, the people holding this hammer ought to be guarded the closest because they have the biggest weapon with which to do either good or evil.

Given people's inherent exploitive nature, as soon as anyone is given unchecked power within society, the FLD are activated. This is exactly what has occurred in many failed societies. Exploiters realized their actions were checked *within* society, so they instead sought control of government's monopoly of force to redirect it toward unjust ends *over* society.

The disgraceful record of poverty in the third world is, in reality, just a long record of rulers' shameful use of government's force hammer for plunder and exploitation. Similarly, Western governments, although less overt than their third-world counterparts, are increasingly unleashing the FLD upon society and unjustly applying the monopoly-of-force hammer. Every government must be set up so that exploiters cannot alter its purpose from protection of justice to protection of injustice.

The FLD challenge within society boils down to this: Whereas government must be given sufficient force to protect society against exploiters, how do the members of society ensure this force isn't captured by exploiters in government and thereby used to plunder them? For any government with the power to restrain injustice also has the power to commit injustice. Every society must consider the FLD when forming government, regardless of the specific type (monarchy, aristocracy, or democracy) chosen, since they constitute an underlying systemic process working upon the human heart. Insofar as all governments are created and led by people, the FLD question (which is based upon human nature) must be addressed, or concord will be short-lived.

Professor Isaac Kramnick of Cornell University captured the challenges inherent within governmental power and the exploitive nature of humans when he wrote the following about the French Revolution and the ideas of Thomas Paine and Edmund Burke:

> Government is simply a necessary evil, useful, if not mandatory, to control ourselves when we fail one another. How we effect that control (and what additional restraints need to be governmentally supported) is for each age to decide. The important consequence for Paine was that no matter how much reverence Burke adduces to support the undeniably important wisdom of the ages, Paine asserts that those living now should not have to forfeit their right to pass judgment on choices made by those no longer alive. Both Paine and Burke decried the extremes of the French Revolution, and both were disillusioned by man's inhumanity to man, but both saw opportunity for needed change in the events unfolding in Paris. Paine's support of the revolution was founded in the insanity of the French monarchy. Burke's denunciation of the revolution was rooted in the insanity of the republic. Both were right.[3]

Kramnick, in essence, argues that any government created by people is susceptible to their strengths (cooperation) and weaknesses (exploitation). The French Revolution, for example, despite overthrowing an inept and unjust monarchy, merely replaced it with an even more inept and unjust democracy that guillotined people in the streets without due process. The French Revolution points to the need for any government seeking justice and concord to address the underlying FLD issues.

But how does a society delegate to the government the monopoly of force to check injustice while still ensuring the government does not become unjust itself? For if exploiters do legally gain control of the government, what would stop them from gradually passing laws to "legalize" plunder for their benefit? Furthermore, how would society object to this increasing oppression when the exploiters in control of the government can use the monopoly of force to intimidate any protesters? Unfortunately, these are not just hypothetical questions. Governments have routinely fallen under the control of exploitive interests. Frédéric Bastiat addressed this specific issue in his classic *The Law*:

> This question of legal plunder must be settled once and for all, and there are only three ways to settle it:
>
> 1. The few plunder the many.
> 2. Everybody plunders everybody.
> 3. Nobody plunders anybody.
>
> We must make our choice among limited plunder, universal plunder, and no plunder. The law can follow only one of these three.[4]

Bastiat believed justice and concord resulted when no one in society was permitted to plunder others by either legal or illegal methods. To check the FLD, government itself must be checked from gaining absolute power over society. Checking the FLD is even more crucial than which specific government (monarchy, aristocracy, or democracy) society utilizes. In reality, all three types can be just or unjust depending upon their success or failure in checking the FLD.

In general, once the FLD are initiated, exploiters seek further expansion of governmental power to increase their ability to plunder. The FLD, simply put, must not be provided fertile ground for growth, or else society is doomed to fall. If this is true, why doesn't society invest the time and energy to develop methods to check the FLD?

There are only two possible answers to this question. First, since few political leaders think systematically, rarely will one intuitively understand the systemic process of the SDS and FLD interacting within society. Accordingly, it may just be ignorance that causes the FLD to grow and the Power Pendulum to move away from concord. If so, the politicians are like the merchant mentioned earlier, who continued to step on a bump in the rug, not realizing the underlying snake was the root cause. The politicians, in effect, settle for the quick-fix, stepping-on-bumps solutions, while they ignore the underlying systemic snakes.

The second possible answer is that political leaders, or those who elect them, know exactly what they are doing. Their policies, in essence, are accomplishing exactly what they intended, namely, more power and plunder for those in control of the state. As exploiters convince society to surrender its power to the state, the state can then hammer society even more for further plunder. Of course, this vicious cycle finally depletes Social Power, and the parasitic State Power dies with its host.

In any event, the goal of this book is to educate political leaders and society's members to recognize the danger in opening the door to the State Power FLD and thereby allowing it to feed off the Social Power SDS. If ignorance is causing the FLD problem, then this book provides the knowledge to achieve concord. If, on the other hand, political design is the cause, then this book alerts society's members to the truth. Armed with that truth, the people can restrain government to its delegated role. Indeed, society will not and cannot achieve justice for all and its quest for concord until the root causes of the FLD are addressed and permanently checked.

Besides Franz Oppenheimer, two more authors were instrumental in helping me discover the systemic root causes behind why all societies fall. Frédéric Bastiat's book *The Law*, already mentioned, drove home that humanity's dual nature (angelic and brutish) must be understood and addressed in order for a healthy society to result. For when either of these natures is emphasized while the other is ignored, one is no longer dealing in reality.

On one side, philosophers can fall into dangerous idealism in believing that, by following a certain course of actions, people can be perfected. Certainly, the illusion of producing the perfected human was shattered by the dismal record of the French and Communist Revolutions.

On the other side, however, philosophers can fall into the equally disastrous pessimism (nihilism) of believing that human beings are incapable of improving themselves and are fated for failure. This false construct of reality has now produced several generations of purposeless, pleasure-seeking automatons who fulfill the expectation of these dreary beliefs by accomplishing nothing. At any rate, Bastiat led me to realize that the best thinkers and political systems take humanity as it is, not as they want it to be. Bastiat's description of people's exploitive nature led me to name the second law in his honor (as we will soon see).

Finally, the last author who contributed to my thinking in developing the FLD was Albert Jay Nock. His systemic descriptions of societal decline assisted greatly, specifically with respect to Gresham's Law and the Law of Diminishing Returns (laws three and four). The writings of Oppenheimer, Bastiat, and Nock paired with my systems engineering background led to the codification of the FLD for depicting the forces behind societal and organizational decline.

Before listing and delving into the laws, a couple of analogies might be helpful in visualizing how the FLD affect society. First, imagine the FLD as five jet nozzles sending water into a swimming pool. Each jet is aimed in the same direction around the perimeter of the pool, thereby causing the current to flow in one direction. Progress in society (hence, the action of the SDS) must move against the current created by the jets. The FLD nozzles are always on, even in a limited government. However, the SDS can overcome the FLD jets so long as the FLD are restrained from increasing their jet nozzle pressure and flow. This will always represent a work of intentional will, as the resistance of the jets will always be there. Of course, if the FLD are not checked, the pressure and flow from the jet nozzles soon overcome the SDS, and society falls.

The second analogy involves the SDS as airplanes and the FLD as gravitational forces. Just as aeronautical engineers must design airplanes to overcome gravity, so too must society design systems of justice to overcome and restrain the FLD. If a government cannot ensure justice for all, the FLD begin to expand. But this FLD growth in society is equivalent to engineers realizing the gravitational constant is increasing. Although airplanes can overcome standard gravitational pull, if gravity's force were doubled, many planes would fall. In a similar fashion, many societies have fallen when the FLD expansions were beyond the capability of the SDS to overcome them.

Take whichever analogy you like. The important thing to visualize is that the FLD are constantly working against the SDS and therefore must be minimized. And this must happen at the same time that the SDS are increased through growing Social Power. With these analogies in mind, it is time to explore the Five Laws of Decline in depth.

CHAPTER FOUR

THE FIVE LAWS OF DECLINE

Without any further ado, the Five Laws of Decline are as follows:

1. **Sturgeon's Law:** 90 percent of the results in every field of human activity are "crud."
2. **Bastiat's Law:** People seek the least amount of exertion required to satisfy their wants.
3. **Gresham's Law:** Unaddressed destructive behaviors drive out productive ones.
4. **Law of Diminishing Returns:** Holding all other variables constant, returns decrease after a certain size of production has been reached.
5. **Law of Inertia:** Once the FLD have been activated within society, it becomes increasingly difficult to stop their deleterious effects and restore justice.

Sturgeon's Law: Leadership Competence

Sturgeon's Law is named in honor of Theodore Sturgeon, one of the top science-fiction writers of his era. In a speech at the 1953 World Science Fiction Convention, Sturgeon addressed one of the main criticisms of the science fiction genre. Evidently, using the worst examples from the field as rationale, many critics had wrongly concluded that science fiction was unscientific garbage.

Sturgeon answered them by articulating a profound truth, not just for science fiction but for all fields associated with human arts. He said 90 percent of science fiction is "crud," but then again, so is 90 percent of *everything*. In a later article in *Venture* magazine, he elaborated upon his principle:

> I repeat Sturgeon's Revelation, which was wrung out of me after twenty years of wearying defense of science fiction against attacks of people who used the worst examples of the field for ammunition, and whose conclusion was that ninety percent of [science fiction] is crud.
>
> Using the same standards that categorize 90% of science fiction as trash, crud, or crap, it can be argued that 90% of film, literature, consumer goods, etc., are crap. In other words, the claim (or fact) that 90% of science fiction is crap is ultimately uninformative, because science fiction conforms to the same trends of quality as all other art forms.[1]

Interestingly, many years before Sturgeon, Benjamin Disraeli had expounded a similar principle with respect to literature when he explained, "Books are fatal: they are the curse of the human race. Nine-tenths of existing books are nonsense, and the clever books are the refutation of that nonsense."[2]

Hence, Sturgeon's Law reveals an important aspect of humanity, namely, that 90 percent of the efforts in any field will be less than stellar. Of course, this principle can be reversed to express that 10 percent of the efforts will be excellent! In reality, this shouldn't be too surprising, since it takes endless hours of study and practice in any field to develop excellence. Look at any profession, and without fail, the cream rises to the top. Some may smear this as elitist, but everyone knows that not all doctors, entertainers, or athletes are equal. Not only is everyone born with different gifts, but there is also a huge discrepancy in the hunger to develop those gifts.

For instance, over the last twenty years, I have built a leadership company. Remarkably, before I had ever heard of Sturgeon's Law, I realized from studying decades' worth of data that most people, although they have leadership capabilities, are not willing to invest the time and effort necessary to become great leaders. Leadership, like other human art forms, requires a person to develop certain qualities (daily diligence, willingness to confront reality, and unyielding persistence, to name a few) in order to rise to the top 10 percent. As a result, the reason the majority of people do not achieve excellence in their given field isn't a lack of talent but a lack of the hunger, focus, and tenacity necessary to reach the upper echelons.

Sturgeon's Law, however, has an even greater implication for the leadership field, including political leadership. As Chris Brady and I described in our book *Launching a Leadership Revolution*, to be a leader, one must simultaneously reach excellence in three specific categories: character, tasks, and relationships. We call this framework the Trilateral Leadership Ledger (TLL), wherein one must develop skills into the top 10 percent in each of the three categories in order to achieve excellence in leadership overall.

People who reach the top 10 percent in only one or two of the areas are still not leaders until they do so in the third.[3]

Therefore, when I combined Sturgeon's Law with the TLL, it confirmed theoretically what I had previously learned experientially, namely, that only one out of a thousand people ever achieve true excellence in the field of leadership. Mathematically, I arrived at one out of a thousand by understanding that, since only 10 percent are excellent in a given area, the number who achieve excellence in all three areas would be 10% x 10% x 10%, or 1/1,000. Rarely do theory and results align so closely, but in this case, the reason Sturgeon's Law is the first law of decline is simply its impressive ability, when married with the Trilateral Leadership Ledger, to predict the number of excellence achievers who will arise in an organization or society.

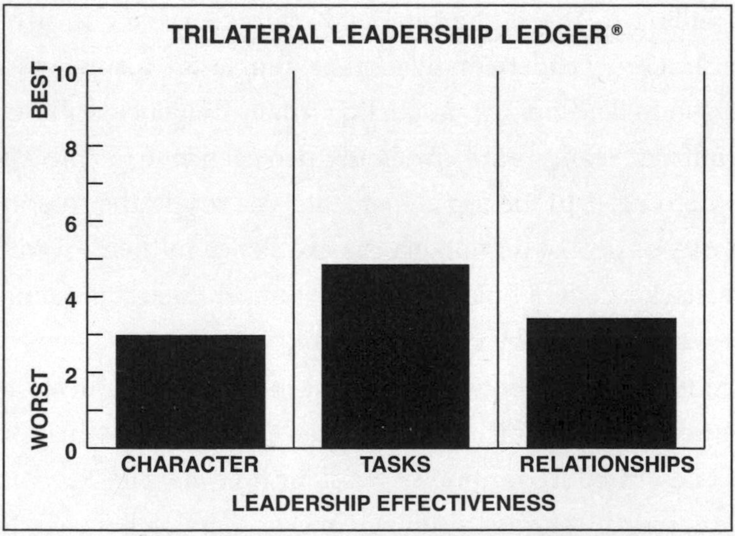

At any rate, if top leadership is present in only about one out of a thousand people, then the chance of a society having a string of top leaders at the helm is a practical impossibility. Therefore, society must have structures and precedents in place to ensure that a poor leader in an important leadership position is not capable of sinking society's ship.

To use a corporate example, imagine where Apple would be today had Steve Jobs not returned to restore its greatness after an eleven-year hiatus. Even though Jobs cofounded Apple, John Scully, the former CEO of Pepsi who had gained control over the Apple board, ousted him. Unimpressed with Jobs's inadequate corporate skills and loose spending, Scully believed Apple would be better off without its cofounder. The marketplace, however, disagreed. Apple stock and profits plummeted over the ensuing years, and many wrote the company off as a lost cause. In fact, after hearing of Jobs's return to Apple, Michael Dell proclaimed what he would do if he were appointed Apple's new CEO: "I'd shut it down and give the money back to shareholders."[4]

Jobs, of course, had a different plan, and his return to the company launched one of the greatest corporate turnarounds in history. Against all odds, Jobs—a one-in-a-thousand (perhaps more like a one-in-a-million) leader—assumed command. He narrowed the focus, reduced corporate costs, and inspired the troops to achieve what others said was impossible. Indeed, the Jobs-led Apple went on to revolutionize three separate industries: computers, music, and cell phones. Can anyone imagine Scully or any other corporate bureaucrat accomplishing this? This is the leadership difference.

Just as in business, true leadership in the political field only amounts to about one in a thousand. Hence, a successful government must be designed to accomplish its delegated objectives even when non-leaders are appointed to key positions. Christopher Bruell described the essence of Sturgeon's Law when he discussed Xenophon's fascinating analysis of the great King Cyrus of Persia:

> Xenophon tells us that he turned his attention to Cyrus after reflecting on the frequency with which democracies, monarchies, oligarchies, and above all, tyrannies are overthrown and reaching the conclusion that it is exceedingly difficult, not to say impossible, for human beings to rule successfully over other human beings. This conclusion seemed to be refuted by the career of Cyrus, which demonstrated that it is neither difficult nor impossible to rule over human beings, provided that one knows how to do it. Cyrus appeared to have solved the political problem. Yet in his conclusion to the *Cyropaedia*, Xenophon admits and even stresses that Cyrus' empire began to fall prey to strife and decay immediately upon his death. The reason is not merely that Cyrus' successors, lacking his great qualities, were unable to maintain the institutions he had established. It is also to be found in the flaws in those institutions themselves.[5]

There are several keys to Bruell's reasoning. First, he pinpoints the essence of Sturgeon's Law when he explains that what seems incredibly difficult to most people (leading a nation) is not beyond the capacity of a true leader. Still, since this level of leadership is extremely rare (one out of a thousand), it cannot endure for long after the true leader is gone. Second, even a true leader cannot, without a thorough understanding of the FLD, build institutions or societies that successfully endure because no one prevents the FLD from growing within once the leader's stabilizing influence has departed. True, while effective leaders are alive, their leadership ability enables them to overcome the systemic defects within the institutional forms, but after their death, these defects become bigger than the leadership capacity of any replacements. The FLD then begin their destructive course.

Therefore, the best governments are founded upon enduring institutions that systematically check the FLD, rather than great temporary leaders (appearing only one out of a thousand times) who will not last. Only permanent institutions that protect against FLD incursions can ensure that the SDS thrive and thereby provide justice for all.

Indeed, one of the greatest dangers for the long-term health of government is when great leaders are permitted to make good decisions but still operate within a flawed structure. Although great leaders can make it work, the bad leaders who will replace them cannot. Society suffers when bad leaders make bad decisions based upon bad precedents. For how can a society stop the bad leaders from applying the same procedures it allowed its great leaders to use? Hence, enduring societal success must be built upon great institutions rather than great leaders.

A modern example of this phenomenon at work is how the United States permitted past presidents to use executive orders to bypass Congress in "emergency situations." This practice has now become the preferred method of presidential power to work around a deadlocked Congress. Even if one believed that the presidential executive orders were justified (which is certainly debatable), few would deny that the precedent set is now routinely abused for State Power gains. Furthermore, since Sturgeon's Law assures that incapable leaders will gain power sooner or later, the bad precedents will soon become the common practice. In consequence, even the best leaders must be restrained institutionally from using improper procedures, since Sturgeon's Law says bad leaders will use these bad precedents to build State Power and weaken Social Power.

Bastiat's Law: Plunder

The linchpin of the Five Laws of Decline is the second one, Bastiat's Law. In effect, much of history is a record of people plundering fellow human beings. Remember that it's human nature to seek to satisfy one's desires with the least amount of effort possible. When society does not ensure that the cooperative "economic means" that create wealth are rewarded and that the antisocial "political means" of wealth expropriation are punished, then most people will be overcome with the temptation to plunder rather than produce. Bastiat described how the internal conflict between people's angelic and brutish natures leads naturally to opposing methods of self-preservation:

> Self-preservation and self-development are common aspirations among all people. And if everyone enjoyed the unrestricted use of his faculties and the free disposition of the fruits of his labor, social progress would be ceaseless, uninterrupted, and unfailing.
>
> But there is also another tendency that is common among people. When they can, they wish to live and prosper at the expense of others. This is no rash accusation. Nor does it come from a gloomy and uncharitable spirit. The annals of history bear witness to the truth of it: the incessant wars, mass migrations, religious persecutions, universal slavery, dishonesty in commerce, and monopolies. This fatal desire has its origin in the very nature of man—in that primitive,

> universal, and insuppressible instinct that impels him to satisfy his desires with the least possible pain.
>
> Man can live and satisfy his wants only by ceaseless labor; by the ceaseless application of his faculties to natural resources. This process is the origin of property.
>
> But it is also true that a man may live and satisfy his wants by seizing and consuming the products of the labor of others. This process is the origin of plunder.
>
> Now since man is naturally inclined to avoid pain—and since labor is pain in itself—it follows that men will resort to plunder whenever plunder is easier than work. History shows this quite clearly. And under these conditions, neither religion nor morality can stop it.
>
> When, then, does plunder stop? It stops when it becomes more painful and more dangerous than labor.[6]

Bastiat, through his extensive study of history, concluded that people will only stop plundering when societal justice causes this avenue to be more painful than production. Otherwise, exploitation increases until the plundering parasite consumes the societal host. Disastrously, although individuals can prosper utilizing either method of wealth accumulation (the cooperative "economic means" or the exploitive "political means"), societies can only prosper when using "economic means" is rewarded and using "political means" is punished.

Interestingly, combining the principles of Sturgeon's Law and Bastiat's Law together reveals that 90 percent of society's members will rationalize exploitation of fellow humans if they can do so without punishment. On the positive side, this also confirms that 10 percent will refuse to sell out their character by choosing the path of plunder. But society cannot survive when only 10 percent behave justly. Accordingly, these two laws together reveal why governments are created and given the monopoly-of-force hammer in society to begin with. For when the 90 percent realize that government will punish them if they apply the unjust "political means" instead of the just "economic means," they will, not surprisingly, avoid the "political means." Consequently, when government performs its delegated role of ensuring justice, the SDS flourish as everyone utilizes the cooperative "economic means" of wealth creation to increase Social Power. In contrast, when government becomes an agent of injustice, the FLD flourish as exploiters utilize the "political means" of wealth expropriation to increase State Power.

A textbook example of Bastiat's Law at work is the Dutch East India Company's entrance into the Banda Islands. Because the Dutch had the overwhelming superiority in force over the Bandanese natives, they chose the easier path of exploitation rather than the more difficult one of production. Although at first the Dutch merely attempted to intimidate the politically divided Bandanese cities into compliance with their monopoly methods, they quickly realized intimidation was not sufficient. Hence, the Dutch, according to Daron Acemoğlu and James A. Robinson, resorted to mass genocide and enslavement to achieve their exploitive ends:

> The Dutch also took control of the Banda Islands, intending this time to monopolize mace and nutmeg. But the Banda Islands . . . were made up of many small autonomous city-states, and there was no hierarchical social or political structure. These small states, in reality no more than small towns, were run by village meetings of citizens. There was no central authority whom the

> Dutch could coerce into signing a monopoly treaty and no system of tribute that they could take over to capture the entire supply of nutmeg and mace. At first this meant that the Dutch had to compete with the English, Portuguese, Indian, and Chinese merchants, losing the spices to their competitors when they did not pay high prices. Their initial plans of setting up a monopoly of mace and nutmeg dashed, the Dutch governor of Batavia, Jan Pieterszoon Coen, came up with an alternative plan. Coen founded Batavia, on the island of Java, as the Dutch East India Company's new capital in 1618. In 1621 he sailed to Banda with a fleet and proceeded to massacre almost the entire population of the islands, probably about fifteen thousand people. All their leaders were executed along with the rest, and only a few were left alive, enough to preserve the know-how necessary for mace and nutmeg production. After this genocide was complete, Coen then proceeded to create the political and economic structure necessary for his plan: a plantation society. . . . These new plantation owners were taught how to produce the spices by the few surviving Bandanese and could buy slaves from the East India Company to populate the now-empty islands and to produce spices, which would have to be sold at fixed prices back to the company.[7]

Despite the shocking nature of this story, it is important to remember that exploitation is a routine occurrence in history, particularly when one group realizes it can reap from another without risk. Entire books could be written on Bastiat's Law as it applies to just the history of South America and Africa. These and other glaring examples confirm that when people believe plunder is easier than production, they rarely have the moral scruples to deny themselves the privilege.

Coen, unfortunately, chose to exploit his power advantage ("political means") over the Bandanese natives rather than cooperate ("economic means") with them. True, the slaughter of 15,000 innocent people resulted from the exploitation, but Coen justified his policies by pointing to his increased profits. As Acemoğlu and Robinson noted, "By the end of the seventeenth century, the Dutch had reduced the world supply of these spices by about 60 percent and the price of nutmeg had doubled."[8] Coen had behaved the way most people do when exploitation is possible, justifying unjust actions by arguing that "the ends justify the means." Of course, there is no legitimate justification for injustice. However, Bastiat's Law does not describe what is right but rather what is true.

Incidentally, the biblical mandate in Matthew 10:16 (KJV) to be "wise as serpents, and harmless as doves" applies here. For until we recognize the plunderous nature of humans, our ignorance leaves us vulnerable to the serpent-like nature of those seeking to reap where they haven't sown. Nevertheless, we must not allow the serpent-like nature within people to make us cynics or, worse yet, exploiters ourselves. The truth of these insights, instead, should set us free by helping us recognize where avenues for potential FLD exploitation are open so we can close them systematically. In essence, the only way to ensure justice within society is for people to learn to be wise as serpents by identifying where the FLD door is open but also harmless as doves by closing the FLD door rather than benefiting from its being open.

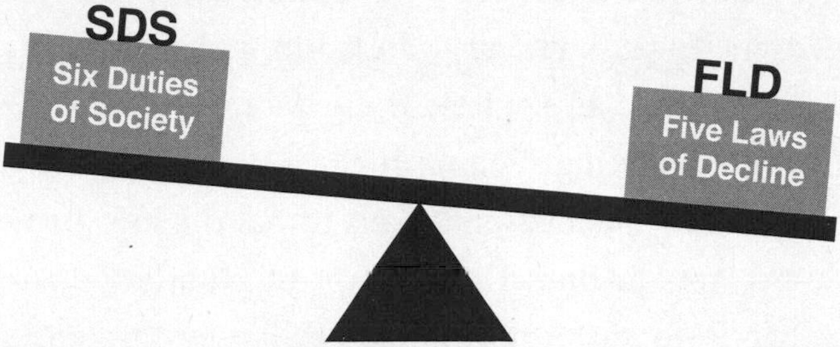

Inevitably, as the FLD increase within society, the SDS decrease proportionally. Therefore, a just society becomes prosperous through the SDS, and an unjust society is damaged by the FLD. Grudem and Asmus expressed the debilitating effects of the unchecked FLD in society when they wrote:

> Officials believe that government jobs are merely a means to enrich themselves and their family and friends. This belief will . . . lead, in many cases, to a kind of "crony capitalism" or an "oligarchic capitalism" in which a small number of very wealthy families are intertwined in close friendships with highly placed government officials, and the government officials will continue to enact policies and distort laws so that their wealthy friends benefit. Then, of course, the wealthy friends will also funnel money back to the highly placed government officials. In such a case, there is little hope for genuine economic growth in the nation as a whole, and almost no hope that the vast majority of people, who are trapped in poverty, will ever make any economic progress.[9]

Alas, as the FLD secure a foothold in society, they become increasingly difficult to eradicate. For although people's needs are limited, their wants appear to be unlimited. Hence, anytime plunder is permitted in society, the exploiters cannot control themselves from wanting even more. In fact, one of the primary reasons communism consistently fails is that the FLD exploiters do not know how to limit the amount of plunder taken from society. That is to say, communism collapses through greed when, as Margaret Thatcher once remarked, the state exploiters "run out of other people's money"[10] to steal. Furthermore, the Socialist societies, where State Power claims to redistribute societal wealth in a fair manner, run into similar problems when those assigned to redistribute the wealth do so to themselves and their cronies.

In fact, anytime a limited government expands beyond its delegated role of defender of internal and external justice, it moves quickly from a limited entity to an unlimited and all-powerful state. State interventions stimulate FLD growth within the SDS as the level of taxation, regulation, and frustration increase within society. Meanwhile, the government assigned to protect society gaining a foothold through Bastiat's Law is analogous to a fox being assigned to protect a chicken coop. In both scenarios, the naive community loses its liberty as the guardian enjoys a series of free meals, while supplies last.

Gresham's Law: Bad Behavior Drives Out Good Behavior

Thomas Gresham, an English financier, described his law of monetary policy when he wrote, "when government compulsorily overvalues one money and undervalues another, the undervalued money will leave the country or disappear into hoards, while the overvalued money will flood into circulation."[11] In short, bad money drives out good money. There are many historical examples of this phenomenon (in *RESOLVED: 13 Resolutions for LIFE,* I discuss colonial New England's disastrous paper money experiment) wherein fiat paper money causes gold and silver specie to disappear from the marketplace. The logic goes like this: Why use anything of *real* value when the state is issuing unbacked paper and using its state hammer (by fiat, or dictate) to call it legal tender? Real money goes into savings as society's members use the fiat paper until the state fraud runs its course.

Gresham's Law, interestingly, can be applied to many other areas besides just the monetary field. For instance, as the "political means" of wealth accumulation grows within society, Gresham's Law works to drive out good politicians, who exit the political field rather than play by the increasingly unjust rules of the game. Once the best potential leaders eliminate themselves from the political process, only the less honorable ones who compromise their character and join the exploiters remain.

Stated most simply, Gresham's Law means what is rewarded increases, while what is punished decreases. In the political arena, if bad character is rewarded and good character punished, society should not be shocked to find so much corruption in politics. Few authors have described the effects of Gresham's Law in the political arena better than Bertrand de Jouvenel:

> Through the prestige of its leaders and the popularity of its principles the group brings victory to its candidates, whom it has chosen less for their personal worth than for the pledge of their obedience to itself; moreover, they will be the more faithful to their party from their inability to make their way without it.

> The first result of this is a degradation of the assembly, which no longer draws its recruits from the best men. . . .
>
> So far the debasement of the electors and the degradation of the assembly are only accidental. They are to become by progressive stages systematized. Syndicates of interest and ambitions will soon take shape which, regarding the assembly as a mere adjunct of Power and the people as a mere cistern for the assembly, will devote themselves to winning votes for the installation of tame deputies who will bring back to their masters the prize for which they have ventured everything, the command of society. . . .
>
> Soon they secured for themselves the selection of the candidates, and, naturally, chose men in their own likeness. . . . From this has followed a prodigious drop in the level of parliaments and in the level of government. . . .
>
> Parliament is then no longer a sovereign assembly in which an elite of independent citizens compare freely formed opinions and so arrive at reasonable decisions. It is now only a clearing-house in which the various parties measure their respective parcels of votes against each other's.[12]

A modern example that demonstrates how Gresham's Law operates in the political process is the impeachment proceedings against President Bill Clinton. Regardless of the party one supports, it should seem odd that an impeachment vote on a morality issue (adultery in the Oval Office) could follow party lines so closely. How could anyone argue that party affiliation is the key factor in determining whether a particular behavior is ethical? Regrettably, if the impeachment proceedings proved anything, it was that party loyalty trumps personal ethics whenever they are in conflict. It appears that Jouvenel's insights into the effects of Gresham's Law from 1945 are even more valid in today's political environment than when he wrote them.

Gresham's Law, to sum up, explains how and why independent thinkers have been driven from the political arena and replaced by obedient servants who follow party mandates.

Law of Diminishing Returns: When Further Investment Produces Decreasing Results

The fourth law, the Law of Diminishing Returns (LDR), is famous in economic history. Dictionary.com defines it as: "a law affirming that to continue after a certain level of performance has been reached will result in a decline in effectiveness."[13] In essence, after a specific point is reached, further investment of resources, assuming all other factors (like capital, knowledge, and effort) are fixed, produces increasingly marginal return.

For instance, imagine a weight lifter who works out for thirty minutes a day. Since he desires further muscle development, he begins exercising an hour per day and achieves improved results. Recognizing that his progress resulted from increasing his time spent in the gym, he adds even more time until, at a certain point, he no longer achieves as much incremental gain. In fact, a point is reached at which more time in the gym actually produces a lower return. The muscles are not allowed the necessary recovery time, and his progress actually reverses. The Law of Diminishing Returns (LDR), in this example, is reached when an added hour no longer produces a higher incremental return in results.

Author Matt Ridley used another example to explain the LDR concept:

> Picking out the pecans from a bowl of salted nuts (a vice of mine) gives diminishing returns: the pieces of pecan in the bowl get rarer and smaller. The fingers keep finding almonds, hazelnuts, cashews, or even—God forbid—Brazil nuts. Gradually the bowl, like a moribund gold mine, ceases to yield decent returns of pecan.[14]

Ridley, because all other variables were constant, had experienced the Law of Diminishing Returns, as each pecan search became progressively less successful.

In the case where the state intervenes in society, the picture is even worse. Not only do society's members not replenish the bowl with their production, but they go further and seek to hide past production from the watchful eyes of the encroaching state. Whereas the SDS apply "economic means" to achieve progressively higher rates of return from improved creativity and production, the FLD, in contrast, apply "political means" and suffer lower rates of return. This is because the state's injustices paralyze societal creativity and production.

State socialism, in a word, believes it can divide the wealth of society equitably, but what actually occurs is that the state uses most of the wealth to feed itself and its cronies, and the LDR ensures the production bowl is not refilled. In such a situation, society fails because its production rapidly diminishes due to an accelerated LDR.

Law of Inertia: Objects "Stay the Course" Until Acted Upon

The Law of Inertia, one of Isaac Newton's thermodynamic laws, states: "Every body remains in a state of rest or uniform motion (constant velocity) unless it is acted upon by an external unbalanced force."[15] In lay terms, an object at rest tends to stay at rest, while an object in motion tends to stay in motion. Entities also maintain their current status until they are acted upon by another force.

For example, imagine several kids in a circular pool running in the same direction. This causes a current to flow with them. When the kids attempt to reverse direction, they struggle against the inertia of the current opposing them. Since the inertia of the pool's current opposes the change in direction, it requires a disciplined effort on the part of the kids in order to reverse the current in the pool. In a similar fashion, leaving the FLD unchecked creates resistance for any leaders seeking to correct injustices within society. Although the leaders may know what to do, they still must battle the inertia of bad precedents, ignorance and apathy, and, above all, the vested interests of those who benefit from the existing injustices. Turnarounds in organizations and societies are, as a result of these inertias, among the toughest of leadership assignments.

This is because bad precedents, once accepted in society, force leaders to run against the accepted practices in an effort to reverse their harmful effects. But few people enjoy being told that their past actions are counterproductive to the new direction. Moreover, it is easier to shoot the messenger than it is to overcome the Law of Inertia created by the bad precedents. Hence, leaders with the courage to educate society's members on the proper course of action must also tactfully explain where society made the wrong turn. This is certainly not an easy task. In fact, although the dream of democracy was built upon the idea of a populace educated about the important issues facing a nation, democratic theory has not lived up to its ideal. As Jouvenel described:

> The fathers of democracy held the view that an election campaign was a season of popular education by means of full exposition of contrary policies; they attached special importance to the publication of parliamentary debates which would, by being reported, enable the citizen to follow the activities of government and so fit him more and more to pass judgment. . . . The fact that the larger spirits would have to solicit the votes of the smaller would mean that the latter, their intelligence once formed in such a school, would at long last be fitted for the leading part which had been assigned to them without exception. Of all the arguments in favor of democracy, this was the noblest.[16]

The theory, unfortunately, failed to take into account Sturgeon's Law and the 90 percent who, through ignorance, apathy, or a combination of both, refuse to think for themselves. Consequently, democratic elections, rather than educating the masses through reasoned arguments, instead digressed into propagandizing through emotional slogans. Jouvenel continued:

> The men of our day, however, being circumspect people, have realized that the cultivation of the elector's intelligence is at least as likely to open a window on the arguments of their opponents as on their own; therefore the labor is lost. The faculty of reason may lie relatively unused in the majority of people, but there is not a man anywhere who is incapable of emotion. And it is to the emotions, therefore, that the appeal must be made. Rouse in your behalf trust, hope, and affection; rouse against your rival indignation, anger, and hatred—and success is yours. It is truly complete when a public meeting can be induced to cheer a speech which it cannot understand,

> and to greet the other side's reply with stampings of the feet. . . . The result is that good citizenship, so far from being awakened among those who are as yet without it, gets extinguished in those who already have it.[17]

Democracy, in effect, has learned the truth of Henry Ford's statement: "Thinking is the hardest work there is, which is probably the reason why so few engage in it."[18] As a result, the political machinery has concluded that it is easier to tell people what to think than to teach them how to think.

Finally, the main reason the Law of Inertia is difficult to overcome within society is because the exploiters have a vested interest in preserving thc status quo. Why, in other words, would the vested interests, who are currently receiving special deals as a result of the unchecked FLD, be interested in surrendering their special privileges? As an example, Acemoğlu and Robinson pinpoint why Africa has had such difficulty in removing extractive institutions since they were firmly established:

> British colonial authorities built extractive institutions in the first place, and the post-independence African politicians were only too happy to take up the baton for themselves. . . . Yet in all these cases, extractive institutions were re-created in a pattern predicted by the vicious circle—only they became more vicious as time went by. . . . Extractive political institutions lead to extractive economic institutions which enrich a few at the expense of many. Those who benefit from extractive institutions thus have the resources to build their [private armies] and mercenaries, to buy their judges, and to rig their elections in order to remain in power. They also have every interest in defending the system. Therefore

> extractive economic institutions create the platform for extractive political institutions to persist. Power is valuable in regimes with extractive political institutions, because power unchecked brings economic riches. Extractive political institutions also provide no checks against abuses of power. Whether power corrupts is debatable, but Lord Acton was certainly right when he argued absolute power corrupts absolutely.[19]

Everyone agrees that Africa is suffering from massive exploitation by state rulers, and unless the state willingly surrenders some of its power to plunder, the Law of Inertia ensures the situation will continue.

This is why the FLD cannot be permitted a foothold within society. For once exploiters receive support from the state, they become vested and resist any proposals for change. The Law of Inertia predicts that the exploiters, because they profit through the control of state machinery, will aggressively defend their privileges to plunder against anyone with the courage to seek justice. The Law of Inertia rounds out the FLD, since it reveals why righting injustice, once it has been permitted to grow within society, becomes an increasingly difficult task. In essence, though Africa may represent an extreme example, it still reveals the love of power and plunder inherent within human beings everywhere. Therefore, when society cracks the door open for FLD exploitation, rest assured, the exploiters' greed will always support its expansion but never its contraction. Regrettably, the Law of Inertia explains why, even when society recognizes it is on the wrong track, the vested interests actively block any attempt to change course and get society back on the right track.

CHAPTER FIVE

THE FIVE LAWS OF DECLINE AND THE THREE FACTORS OF PRODUCTION

Now that we have studied how the Six Duties of Society and the Five Laws of Decline work individually, it is time to consider how they interact with one another to affect people's inalienable rights within the state–society framework. It's probably obvious by this point that I believe the free market can solve society's challenges by using persuasion and innovation, as long as governments ensure justice for all. There are many different labels for this system, such as *free market*, *free enterprise*, and *capitalism*, but I like the term *free market* the best. For capitalism (capital ownership, investment opportunities, and profits) can exist in a command economy as easily as in a free economy. Thus, when people use the term *capitalism*, the nebulous meaning of that term muddles the thinking and dialogue. I believe free-market solutions to society's challenges through the use of persuasion and innovation are much more effective for maximizing the SDS and minimizing the FLD than any centralized command-and-control structure that damages the SDS and feeds the FLD. And I believe the term *free market* is the most accurate description of that condition.

Johan Norberg expresses the difference between free (SDS) and command (FLD) economies clearly:

> What I am defending, then, is individual liberty in the economy. Capitalists are dangerous, when, instead of seeking profit through competition, they join forces with government. If the state is a dictatorship, corporations can easily be parties to human rights violations, as a number of Western oil companies have been in African states. By the same token, capitalists who stalk the corridors of political power in search of benefits and privileges are not true capitalists. On the contrary, they are a threat to the free market and as such must be criticized and counteracted. Often, businessmen want to play politics, and politicians want to play at being businessmen. That is not a market economy; it is a mixed economy in which entrepreneurs and politicians have confused their roles. Free capitalism exists when politicians pursue liberal policies and entrepreneurs do business.[1]

Here Norberg beautifully describes the difference between an SDS economy and an FLD-infected one. The only way for society to achieve justice for all and societal concord is to deny the elites the power and means to exploit society.

Bertrand de Jouvenel once shared a sobering perspective on the history of humankind that has ramifications for both the SDS and FLD:

> Whoever does not wish to render history incomprehensible by departmentalizing it—political, economic, social—would perhaps take the view that it is in essence a battle of dominant wills, fighting in every way they can for the material which is common to everything they construct: the human labor force.[2]

Jouvenel didn't use the terms *FLD* and *SDS*, but he certainly described the effects of both wonderfully. For if the FLD truly drive the elites to control the production of the masses, they must do so by exploiting the three inputs of all production (labor, land, and capital) as outlined by the classical economists such as Smith, Ricardo, and Mill. One can confirm the validity of the FLD by realizing that the elites, in order to exploit the masses' production, must exploit labor, land, or capital, since these are the only three inputs for all production. As explained below, a person would be hard-pressed to find another example where theory matches reality more closely than the FLD theory matches the actions of the world's exploiters.

The FLD exploitation of the masses' production by elites originated with the elites controlling the masses' labor (physical slavery) to control production. Indeed, for thousands of years, this was the preferred method of control. Over time, however, this method fell out of favor as Christianity permeated Roman society. As it became increasingly intolerable for Christians to enslave fellow Christians (regrettably, enslaving non-Christians was still tolerable), the exploiters switched to the second factor of production, land. Instead of physical slavery, the masses now endured land serfdom, as the elites owned and controlled the land. The elites' direct ownership of the land gave them indirect ownership of the people. Fortunately for the people, however, as the free-market system blossomed, they were no longer beholden to the land-owning aristocracy for survival and were increasingly able to prosper through private enterprise and businesses of their own.

It is not hard to guess what the elites did next, given that there was only one input of production (capital) left to control. As predicted, when feudalism had run its course and private enterprise began to spread, the battle between state and society for the control of capital commenced. Although society at first successfully created a gold standard (which checked the state's ability to control the monetary system), the elite statists eventually regained the upper hand. The state (always hungry for funds to increase its power) finally wrestled money away from the FLD-restraining gold standard and became capital's sole creator, owner, and controller. They did this through the artifices of the central banking system's centralized planning of the money supply. By directly controlling the monetary system, the elites indirectly control the masses' production, since nearly everyone uses capital (the third input of all production) in today's money economies. The exploitation of capital by the elites confirms in practice what a study of the FLD and its interaction with the three factors of production predicted in theory.

The elites have progressively used the FLD to exploit the masses' production through physical slavery, land serfdom, and finally financial subjugation. Moreover, each time the FLD moved to the next production factor, the elites were given an even more effective exploitation tool, since exploitation increases as the quantity of production to be plundered increases. When people realize they are enslaved, they barely work above sustenance. Serfdom, on the other hand, at least allowed people to keep a percentage of their production, and therefore productivity naturally remained at a decent level. Above all, however, is financial subjugation, which gives people the illusion that they are free, even though interest and inflation exploit them as slavery and serfdom did their ancestors.

How does the manipulation of the money supply enslave society? The answer can be seen when one understands the process. The central banks create money out of thin air electronically, and this new money is then loaned to people who buy nonimaginary items such as cars, houses, and entertainments. (The money is first loaned to other banks and big business cronies in cahoots with the central bank authorities and is therefore spendable before the resulting inflationary effects have yet taken root.) Interest is then paid to the banks for this "fiat" money that they do not actually possess but have loaned out nonetheless! Further, every time the central banking system creates more fiat money out of thin air, the flow of all that new money into the marketplace has the effect of raising prices for consumers. This is because more and more money is fighting for the same amount of goods. In such a market, it is not long before sellers realize a higher price can be obtained for their goods. The net result of this inflationary policy on the part of the central banks is that everyone's savings correspondingly *decrease* in value because as prices go up, the purchasing power of their money goes down. As the government manufactures more instant money for its own purposes, the savings of the hardworking people on the street are stolen invisibly through this process.

In effect, the state has permitted the centralized banks to have the FLD sweetheart deal of the millennium, since they receive interest on fake money that must be paid for by the real productive efforts of society's members. In addition, the state benefits from supporting the centrally planned banking system since it is permitted to borrow copious amounts of fiat money to increase its own power over society. Sure, it runs up huge deficits yearly, and the government debt grows astronomically as a result, but the state isn't worried because it is society that must service the debt. Plus, the politicians know they will be out of office before the "chicken hits the fan" and the problem is pushed on to the next generation anyway. Finally, since hardly anyone in society is aware of the destructive effects caused by the state's partnership with the central banking system, the money manipulation is either unnoticed or, even more peculiarly, praised by those in financial subjugation.

At any rate, the FLD control over the masses throughout history has progressed from "owning" the people to control the production of society, to "owning" the land to control production, and then finally to "owning" the capital to control production. The FLD are not just theoretical. Elites have fed off society's production since humans first formed societies. And although the methods of exploitation are certainly less direct now than in the past, they are much more effective because they are less detectable.

Near the end of his nonagenarian life, Nobel Prize–winning economist F. A. Hayek summarized the state's destructive role in the market:

> Under government patronage the monetary system has grown to great complexity, but so little private

> experimentation and selection among alternative means has ever been permitted that we still do not quite know what good money could be—or how good it could be. Nor is such interference and monopoly a recent creation: it occurred almost as soon as coinage was adopted as a generally accepted medium of exchange. Though an indispensable requirement for the functioning of an extensive order of cooperation of free people, money has almost from its first appearance been so shamelessly abused by governments that it has become the prime source of disturbance of all self-ordering processes in the extended order of human cooperation. The history of government management of money has, except for a few short happy periods, been one of incessant fraud and deception. In this respect, governments have proven far more immoral than any private agency supplying distinct kinds of money in competition possibly could have been.[3]

The state, in essence, builds an FLD monetary hammer where society had once built an SDS monetary haven.

It is important for anyone seeking justice for all in society to understand how the SDS and FLD interact. Only then can one understand how state policies, procedures, and programs affect the growth of the FLD. Indeed, until an enduring method for restraining the FLD is developed, the quest for concord will remain an unfulfilled dream.

CHAPTER SIX

HOW THE FIVE LAWS ATTACK THE SIX DUTIES

As we have repeatedly discussed, governments have a tried-and-true method for building State Power: intervening within the SDS to consume Social Power. Any time the state intervenes in the SDS, it creates injustices where it is supposed to be deterring them. The state, unfortunately, routinely increases its power by passing laws for the state to do what it would punish individuals for doing. Hence, law is perverted in order to increase State Power.

The state's preferred method for gaining power is through promising to help society fulfill its duties by intervening in the SDS. Of course, it is incapable of helping society fulfill the SDS outside of its delegated defense duty, but it doesn't let that fact get in the way of its love for power. As a consequence, the state has developed creative methods of intervention in every part of the SDS. Because the state is always short on the funds needed to feed its voracious appetite for power, the extent to which it has intervened within the sphere of the SDS should surprise no one.

Let's examine each of the Six Duties of Society and see how the state intervenes to gain funding and power.

The Six Duties of Society

Physical

1. Distribution
2. Division of Labor
3. Duplication of Members
4. Defense

Metaphysical

5. Distinction (on Performance)
6. Dreams (Vision and Goals)

Distribution

Exchange and Tariffs

The state employs many methods to exploit the distribution duty. One technique is to place tariffs on any goods entering, and sometimes exiting, its domain. This increases the price for consumers as the merchants must add the tariff onto the price of the products. Paradoxically, the state assigned to protect its members has, through enforcing a tariff on incoming goods, effectively blockaded its ports in order to raise state revenues at the expense of society's members. Blockades are considered an act of war designed to lessen the will of a society to resist by causing product shortages and raising prices. With a tariff, the state has essentially declared war on the members of its own society. Moreover, when tariffs are used, not to raise a limited tax, but to protect local businesses from foreign competition, the FLD are let loose upon society. For those few served by the tariffs will petition government to raise them even higher so they can sell their merchandise well above the market rate. The state, in other words, has used its monopoly of force to benefit a few businesses at the expense of society's members. This violates the inalienable rights of society by plundering the property of the many to increase that of the few. Plus, the resultant reduced trade decreases capital accumulation and damages the SDS.

Unfortunately, the state has rarely overcome the urge to increase taxes when it has been given the ability to do so. Thus the state's siphon consumes Social Power's capital, and a negative sum (diminishing returns) scenario results where the State Power grows and Social Power fades away. Ridley describes how this process has existed since ancient times:

> In . . . Bronze Age empires commerce was the cause, not the symptom of prosperity. Nonetheless, a free trade area lends itself easily to imperial domination. Soon, through tax, regulation, and monopoly, the wealth generated by trade was being diverted into the luxury of the few and the oppression of the many. By 1500 BC you could argue that the richest parts of the world had sunk into the stagnation of palace socialism as the activities of the merchants were progressively nationalized. Egyptian, Minoan, Babylonian, and Shang dictators ruled over society with extravagant bureaucracy and feeble individual rights, stifling technological innovation, crowding out social innovation, and punishing creativity.[1]

Social Power, in other words, was buried under the weight of omnipresent and omnivorous State Power. The state, outside of imposing a limited tariff to cover the cost of ensuring the inalienable rights of its members, should not permit tariffs to be an avenue of growth for the FLD.

Income Tax

Income tax has proven to be the goose that lays the golden eggs for government. Although every government, even one performing its limited and delegated role, needs constant funding, the invention of income tax has led to the unlimited state. Indeed, expecting a limited government to restrain itself when it has been handed the power to tax the people's income indiscriminately is like expecting alcoholics to restrain their drinking when they have a free pass for unlimited drinks from the local brewery.

It cannot be emphasized enough that power is an irresistible drug, and money is its means of purchase. Hence, any government given a practically unlimited ability to tax will use this power over the purse to build State Power by taxing Social Power. The state's view of society is akin to a shepherd over his sheep, namely, seeking to shear them as closely as possible without slaughtering them.

Montesquieu articulated the temptation for growing State Power as follows:

> The revenues of the state are a portion that each subject gives of his property in order to secure or to have agreeable enjoyment of the remainder. To fix these revenues in a proper manner, regard should be had both

> to the necessities of the state and those of the subject. The real wants of the people ought never to give way to the imaginary wants of the state. Imaginary wants are those which flow from the passions, and from the weakness of the governors, from the charms of an extraordinary project, from the distempered desire of vainglory and from a certain impotency of mind incapable of withstanding the attacks of fancy. Often has it happened that ministers of a restless disposition have imagined that the wants of the state were those of their own little ignoble souls.[2]

The state and society have long had an ongoing dispute over the definition of appropriate, equitable, and just levels of taxation. Indeed, when John Marshall wrote that "the power to tax is the power to destroy,"[3] he reminded us why limiting government's ability to tax is just as important as limiting its sphere of operation. In fact, the only proven method for limiting the state has been limiting its funds. For any time the funds have been available to do so, government's force hammer has routinely gone outside its delegated boundary to become the exploiters' agent of injustice. Taxation has typically been used by rulers to optimize their profits and power by providing special deals for the few funded by increased taxation upon the many. Tax historian Charles Adams wrote:

> A government that taxes excessively is like a spouse that engages in adultery. Its destructiveness is usually not apparent until it is too late. . . . A society can best be evaluated by examining who is taxed, what is taxed, and how taxes are assessed, collected, and spent. Those in

> control of the political process invariably bear lighter tax burdens than those on the outside. . . . Taxes are forced exactions. The loss of money through taxation often enrages people and drives them to revolt. Governments, therefore, must face their tax management with the utmost prudence and wisdom. . . . A government that shackles its people with grossly inequitable tax laws and despotic enforcement practices loses all moral persuasion with respect to compliance, and can hardly complain if its taxpayers resort to all kinds of schemes to protect themselves. . . . The ethics then, of society's tax policy should develop from two moral maxims: First, it is the duty—the first duty—of every government to develop just and sound revenue systems. . . . Second, it is the duty of every person to pay his (or her) fair share of the costs of maintaining the government that serves and protects them.[4]

Regrettably, the history of taxation reveals the inability of those in power to lightly shear society's sheep. As the tax rates increase, the shearing transforms into slaughter as the people are mercilessly plundered. Moreover, the increased taxes rob the people of the capital needed to grow the SDS. As a result, societal growth slows and begins its inevitable decline.

Although people can endure injustices for extended periods of time, they will not tolerate an unjust tax system indefinitely. If the FLD continue to expand because of the tax system, then evasion, exile, and rebellion become the potential paths of action. But when the rebellion against the state's oppression reaches a certain point, the SDS collapse as either chaos or coercion overthrows societal concord.

Capital Manipulation/Inflation

A third way that government intrudes into the distribution duty is through the manipulation of the monetary system. Evidently, even though government's avariciousness for money to grow its power has been well documented historically, society has somehow concluded it can trust government to control the money supply. Unfortunately, nothing has been more fatal to the inalienable rights of society's members than its misplaced trust in government as regards monetary policy. In fact, society might just as well trust a drug addict with an unlimited supply of contraband before it should entrust the inevitably power-hungry and money-poor state (and its cronies) to control the money supply.

Recall our discussion on the creation of money that demonstrated money originated from the free-market process of bartering, not from state fiat and control. Thus, since society created gold and silver coins freely in the SDS, the state should not control what it didn't create. In effect, the state's only valid function is the same as in every other area of free society, namely, to ensure justice for all parties by protecting inalienable rights. With respect to gold and silver coins, government's true role is to ensure an honest Bureau of Standard Weights and Measures to protect against fraudulent debasement of the money supply.

Unfortunately, as Murray Rothbard described, the state has routinely violated the inalienable rights of its members by abusing its delegated responsibility:

> The problem is that governments have systematically betrayed their trust as guardians of the precisely defined weight of the money commodity. If government sets

> itself up as the guardian of the international meter or the standard yard or pound, there is no economic incentive for it to betray its trust and change the definition. For the Bureau of Standards to announce suddenly that 1 pound is now equal to 14 instead of 16 ounces would make no sense whatever. There is, however, all too much of an economic incentive for governments to change, especially to lighten, the definition of the currency unit; say, to change the definition of the pound sterling from 16 to 14 ounces of silver. This profitable process of the government's repeatedly lightening the number of ounces or grams in the same monetary unit is called debasement.[5]

The government, assigned by society to ensure justice through protecting against the debasement of society's money, has instead monopolized the monetary system so it can debase it itself! Because society remains ignorant of this systematic monetary fraud, it permits the state to have unlimited access to fiat money in its ongoing efforts to tamper with the SDS and feed State Power.

Monetary manipulation is, in fact, the biggest area where the Five Laws of Decline have infected the SDS. State Power gains, while Social Power foots the entire bill through the inflationary loss of money's purchasing power, increased taxes, and the boom/bust cycle. The government clearly recognizes the fraudulent nature of counterfeiting, since it hammers any other counterfeiters with the temerity to compete against its monopoly position in the trade. Still, somehow the state has deluded society into believing that, even though it is shamefully wrong for people to counterfeit individually, it is perfectly acceptable for the state to counterfeit corporately. Furthermore, since it is difficult to track where the inflation is coming from, it is one of the state's safest methods for plundering society. As Rothbard observed:

> Direct, overt taxation raises hackles and can cause revolution; inflationary increases of the money supply can fool the public—its victims—for centuries. Only when its paper money has been accepted for a long while is the government ready to take the final inflationary step: making it irredeemable, cutting the link with the gold. After calling its dollar bills equivalent to 1/20 gold ounce for many years, and having built up the customary usage of the paper dollar as money, the government can then boldly and brazenly sever the link with gold, and then simply start referring to the dollar bill as money itself. Gold then becomes a mere commodity, and the only money is paper tickets issued by the government. The gold standard has become an arbitrary fiat standard. The government, of course, is now in seventh heaven. So long as paper money was redeemable in gold, the government had to be careful how many dollars it printed. If, for example, the government has a stock of $30 billion in gold, and keeps issuing more paper dollars redeemable in that gold, at a certain point, the public might start getting worried and call upon the government for redemption. If it wants to stay on the gold standard, the embarrassed government might have to contract the number of dollars in circulation: by spending less than it receives, and buying back and burning the paper notes. No government wants to do anything like that.[6]

The state has also, in effect, created a centralist planning board over the nation's money supply. Despite the repeated failures of the centralist planners in the Eastern European states, it appears the state has ignored these valuable lessons as it pertains to monetary policy. Even Alan Greenspan, the former Federal Reserve chairman, readily admits that centralist planning is a hopelessly incompetent, inefficient, and ineffective method for societal organization when compared to the free market. Nonetheless, the state and its cronies have somehow concluded that, despite the dismal record of centralist planning throughout history, central banks are the best method for structuring monetary matters within society.

Perhaps it's time to reevaluate the state's conclusions with respect to monetary policies, especially when one considers the catastrophic inflationary results and boom/bust cycles suffered since the formation of the Federal Reserve in 1913. Economist Kevin Dowd concurs:

> There is mounting evidence that the monetary instability created by the Federal Reserve—persistent and often erratic inflation, the unpredictable shifts of Federal Reserve monetary policy, and the gyrating interest rates that accompany both inflation and the monetary policy that creates it—have inflicted colossal damage on the U.S. economy and on the fabric of American society more generally. Furthermore, much as the United States has suffered, less fortunate countries have suffered far more. Most of us have watched in horror, for example, as Russia has come out of more than seventy years of Communist misery only to slide now into the abyss of hyperinflation. Unlike some disasters, monetary instability is entirely

> avoidable, but to avoid it, we need to make sure that the monetary system is built on the right foundations—foundations we are very far from having.[7]

Even with the dismal results of the centrally planned banking model, it is highly unlikely that the state will surrender its control of the money supply. Perhaps the state's refusal to follow a free-market course in monetary matters has less to do with ideological fervor than it does its centrally planned source of fiat funds used to feed further interpositions into the SDS.

Thomas Jefferson recognized the risk of state control over the money supply and argued against it in the 1809 debates for the Bank Bill recharter. In 1814, he wrote the following in a letter to Thomas Cooper:

> Everything predicted by the enemies of banks, in the beginning, is now coming to pass. We are to be ruined now by the deluge of bank paper. It is cruel that such revolutions in private fortunes should be at the mercy of avaricious adventurers, who, instead of employing their capital, if any they have, in manufactures, commerce, and other useful pursuits, make it an instrument to burden all the interchanges of property with their swindling profits, profits which are the price of no useful industry of theirs.[8]

Increasingly, inflation siphons away the purchasing power of money to benefit the state at society's expense. Since the monetary policies are in the absolute control of the state (and its cronies), the state can expand or depress the money supply at will, giving the FLD unlimited access to benefit or bankrupt any person, business, or power base within society. This is nothing less than the complete negation of the inalienable rights of society's members. Perhaps the simplest way to explain this is to ask the question: Is it truly wise to permit any group in society to have an unchecked power over the livelihood of the rest of its members? Anyone with even a basic understanding of the FLD would answer the question with an emphatic "No."

If this is so, then why do we constantly hear the state, universities, and media expound upon the importance of central banks in protecting against monetary collapse? Simply stated, governments promote monetary sophisms to disguise their schemes to control and systematically exploit society's members through manipulation of the nation's money supply. Without public acceptance of the state's control over the monetary system, the FLD would not be allowed to intervene as freely into the SDS. Interestingly, through controlling the political parties, media sources, and educational institutions, the state (with its cronies) has poured out copious amounts of monetary misinformation into society. The reason, of course, is to thoroughly confuse the exploited masses while discrediting those who detect the deceit. It is this mass ignorance of the monetary facts that have imperiled society's inalienable rights. The state propaganda essentially argues that, since all production is good and increases wealth, the state must increase the money supply to enable the increase in societal wealth. The fallacy, however, is that unlike all other consumer goods, money is not used up in the consumption or production process. True, it is indispensable to both steps, but only as a medium of exchange for goods and services. Rothbard remarks:

> Unlike consumer or capital goods, we cannot say that the more money in circulation the better. In fact, since money

> only performs an exchange function, we can assert . . . that any supply of money will be equally optimal with any other. In short, it doesn't matter what the money supply may be; every [amount] will be just as good as any other for performing its cash balance exchange function.[9]

In other words, society can practically use any stable non-manipulated money supply level in its role as a medium of exchange for all goods and services. Exploiters reject this economic truth, for if it were accepted within society, it would end the FLD manipulation of the money supply. Hence, the state utilizes every means at its disposal to gain control of a nation's money in order to exploit society.

Ludwig von Mises, who successfully explained (1) why communism would collapse over sixty years before it actually did, (2) how society's boom/bust economic cycle resulted from the state's monetary inflation, and (3) why the state is dangerous for liberty and prosperity, also wrote of the conflict of interest between the state, society, and big banking institutions:

> But even if the 100 percent reserve plan were to be adopted on the basis of the unadulterated gold standard, it would not entirely remove the drawbacks inherent in every kind of government interference with banking. What is needed to prevent any further credit expansion is to place the banking business under the general rules of commercial and civil laws compelling every individual and firm to fulfill all obligations in full compliance with the terms of the contract. If banks are preserved as privileged establishments subject to special legislative provisions, the tool remains that governments can use

> for fiscal purposes. Then every restriction imposed upon the issuance of fiduciary media depends upon the government's and the parliament's good intentions. They may limit the issuance for periods which are called normal. The restriction will be withdrawn whenever a government deems that an emergency justifies resorting to extraordinary measures.[10]

Anything less, and the exploiters, through controlling the expansion and contraction of credit, can profit by this foreknowledge to siphon off wealth from society. Indeed, the greatest challenge to the inalienable rights and justice in the modern world is the unchecked FLD state control over the money supply.

Ironically, although the money supply is the most dangerous area in which to open the door to the FLD, it is, in fact, the area of society where the state and its cronies appear to be trusted the most. In effect, they have been given absolute control to manipulate the money supply at their discretion. As a result, the non-angelic state rulers open the FLD door, and society is expropriated of its wealth without its consent or knowledge.

Division of Labor

The division of labor duty is adversely affected by the FLD when excessive taxation drains needed capital from economic expansion. Moreover, the state also piles on various regulations (minimum wages, health care, and Social Security, to name a few) which also hurt expansion. Since most new jobs are created by small businesses, when excessive taxation and regulations drain capital accumulations, the ability of small businesses to hire more people and increase specialization is reduced.

The state should not be involved in contracts between free parties. If either side is unhappy or believes it is not being treated fairly, it can walk away from the negotiating table. Indeed, when the state gets involved in bargaining, the force hammer comes into play, and Social Power is surrendered to the growing State Power. Employers do not need to be forced into hiring more people if they are accumulating capital by making a profit. Furthermore, so long as numerous firms are competing for limited employees, the division of labor will grow as people freely choose career paths that optimize their needs, goals, and dreams.

Justice for all, the only proper sphere of government within the SDS, ensures that all people's inalienable rights are protected so they are free to pursue the career path of their choosing without coercion of any kind outside of the rule of law (justice).

Duplication

The duplication duty of society is also best satisfied without any government interference. Since couples naturally desire to marry, have children, and build families, the best policy for government is to protect inalienable rights and let society's members determine population growth. Couples will use their liberty to determine family sizes on their own without state mandates.

Unfortunately, governments across the world have interfered with this duty in many different ways. At first, since a growing population helps grow the division of labor, the aristocratic exploiters encouraged population growth. The state used slogans of national greatness, pride in the motherland or fatherland, and even tax breaks to coax population growth during the nineteenth and twentieth centuries. Because Western society during this period was heavily influenced by classical liberalism, the intense competition experienced between Western societies caused most of the states to encourage the people to increase population levels in an effort to satisfy the SDS better than their neighboring states.

Curiously, however, Western society's view on population growth transformed after the welfare state came into being. Indeed, no longer was the state openly promoting population growth, as concerns about the cost of feeding the overpopulating earth took center stage. Not surprisingly, this thinking led to the end of Western society's post-WWII population boom, and population growth ended when later-in-life marriages, increasing divorce rates, and abortion on demand entered the equation. In fact, some states, in a blatant violation of their citizens' inalienable rights, intervened directly in the duplication duty to halt population growth. For instance, both China and India have used State Power to coerce families into limiting the amount of children per family. Although no state in Western civilization has yet issued any mandates on family size, the notion that the state has the right to interfere with the duplication duty appears to be growing.

Apparently, as the FLD increase within society, the state examines population growth pragmatically to determine whether an increasing or decreasing population is better for those ruling the state. If State Power has declared the Law of Diminishing Returns applicable to population growth, the state will seek to slow its growth. On the other hand, if Social Power is growing, and increased population increases the state's overall power, then the state encourages it. The state, in a sense, has launched the FLD into the duplication duty to influence families on how many children they should have. This is a prime example of government becoming the worst violator of the citizens' inalienable rights that it was established to protect.

Unfortunately, however, the state interferes with population growth in a much more significant way than mentioned previously. The Five Laws of Decline predict (and history confirms) that when a state has the power to exploit a weaker nation's wealth for its gain, it usually does so. The politics of power push the state to maximize its power, and as Carl von Clausewitz once wrote, "War is politics by other means."[11] Therefore, when a state believes it can enhance its power by attacking its weaker neighbor, war results. In general, when one state believes it has the power to plunder without penalty and the other has products to pillage without protection, then Clausewitz's dictum is applied. Even though war is an unjust aggression of one nation against another, the FLD temptation of the stronger nation to increase its power, plunder, and prestige at the expense of the weaker is difficult to resist. Nothing, in fact, has damaged the duplication duty more than the state's unceasing urge for more power.

Inconceivably, the government has used its delegated monopoly of force designed to protect society from internal and external aggression to instead usurp another nation's sovereignty unjustly. Regardless of the rhetoric, when one country invades another, there is almost always an underlying political motive revolving around power and plunder. The limited government that continuously interferes with the SDS will eventually become an all-powerful state seeking to gain power at its weaker neighbor's expense. Of course, the weaker nation will attempt to defend itself, and the resulting conflict will damage the life, liberty, and property of both societies. Like the old saying, "When elephants fight, grass dies," both societies lose grass (Social Power) when the elephants (State Powers) battle for supremacy. Ironically, the former limited government created to protect the life, liberty, and property of its society's members has been transformed into a powerful state that attacks the life, liberty, and property of another society's members.

It isn't just the weaker society's members who suffer injustice. For the increased State Power to commit injustices against the weaker nation is paid for by the loss of life, liberty, and property (Social Power) of the aggressor. This point cannot be emphasized enough! Simply stated, neither society wins in war because only State Power increases for the winner, while Social Power is lost in both societies. Indeed, the only "winners" are the individual winning state rulers who have gained through plundering the power, prestige, and purse of the losing state. By contrast, members in both societies have lost portions of their inalienable rights as State Power increased to battle the opponent. Of course, the defeated society loses life, liberty, and property, but what cannot be overlooked is that the victorious society has suffered similar losses. For when the state goes to war, it does so by sacrificing the lives of society's members to achieve its military objectives, making "reasons of state" more important than inalienable rights. This turns society into a tool of the state rather than the limited government being society's tool. Liberty is sacrificed on the altar of regimentation as the state consumes Social Power to defeat the "enemy." Perhaps it's time to realize that unjust attacks upon other societies make the homeland state the real enemy, not the weaker foreign nation. To top it off, the plunder paid for by the sacrifice of the life, liberty, and property of society's members is not shared with society but rather reserved for the state and its cronies.

Is anyone truly willing to argue, from an inalienable rights perspective, that the victorious State Power increase is worth the loss of Social Power and the subsequent loss of life, liberty, and property through war casualties, increased regimentation, and increased taxation in society? Although war certainly appears to build State Power for the victorious rulers, society's members unjustly pay for it. Thus, offensive wars waged by power-hungry FLD rulers must be checked by society, or the nation will quickly change from a limited government to an all-powerful state.

Indeed, it has been the repeated failure to check the FLD in this crucial area that has caused the downfall of so many once-free societies. For unjust offensive wars are, in truth, lose–lose propositions causing the loss of inalienable rights for societies' members on both sides. Meanwhile, the state gains through the further consolidation of its power. In conclusion, then, it is the unchecked rise of the FLD that leads to the fall of the SDS as State Power accumulates and Social Power evaporates.

Defense

Defense against internal and external aggression is the only area of the SDS where government's monopoly of force is needed. Government must have sufficient force to check exploitation, or injustice will flourish in society. Government's internal defense uses its force, limited by the rule of law, to ensure that society is provided justice for all. Unfortunately, however, this force can be conveniently converted by the active FLD into "plunder by law." Once again, Bastiat described the danger of exploiters using the law for unjust ends:

> The law has gone further than this; it has acted in direct opposition to its own purpose. The law has been used to destroy its own objective: It has been applied to annihilating the justice that it was supposed to maintain; to limiting and destroying rights which its real purpose was to respect. The law has placed the collective force at

> the disposal of the unscrupulous who wish, without risk, to exploit the person, liberty, and property of others. It has converted plunder into a right, in order to protect plunder. And it has converted legitimate defense into a crime, in order to punish legitimate defense. . . . It is impossible to introduce into society a greater change and a greater evil than this: the conversion of the law into an instrument of plunder.[12]

The active FLD unleashed upon society will cause exploiters to seek plunder by creating laws that legalize theft from the many for the gain of the few. But when the law is abused in this way, the government, designed to ensure justice, becomes the enforcer of injustice, and the SDS suffer the consequences. The members of society soon redirect their energies from "economic means" of wealth creation to "political means" of wealth expropriation, damaging Social Power and the SDS, and finally collapsing society.

Government's external defense should be limited by the natural law among nations to ensure justice for all. In fact, the only justifiable act of force against another nation is to defend society against an aggressive act by the other. Otherwise, free markets and free exchange should be the norm as nations seek win–win scenarios that build good will rather than lose–lose ones that cause strife. Sadly, when power increases in government, its posture with respect to other nations can change from defense to offense. This is especially evident when it seeks to either directly exploit a weaker nation or support the international financial and corporate behemoths in their overseas expansion by providing "police" services at the taxpayers' expense. Although international businesses can be risky due to the culture and character of foreign rulers and populaces, it is still unacceptable for corporations to expect their government (paid for by society's members) to ensure justice abroad.

Why, in other words, should the tax dollars of society's members be used to ensure profits for foreign investments of any particular company? Instead, the corporation should take into consideration the local government's ability to ensure justice and invest accordingly. All contracts should be enforced through adjudication, with the threat of governmental force for noncompliance coming from the local government, not a corporation's home government. Moreover, who would say the weaker society receives justice when the stronger nation's military is the judge, jury, and enforcement arm for its nation's business interests? Without a neutral third-party judge, the clear danger is that the weaker society's members will become financially enslaved by the unjust partnership between local tyrants and international business conglomerates.

To ensure justice for all, the goal of an ethical society should be to make plunder of all types illegal. This is possible only when the law returns to its proper function of penalizing injustice, rather than promoting it. In conclusion, although plunder is unjust at all times, there are both legal and illegal varieties. Bastiat described the two types of plunder:

> I do not think that illegal plunder, such as theft or swindling—which the penal code defines, anticipates, and punishes— . . . systematically threatens the foundations of society. Anyway, the war against this kind of plunder has not waited for the command of these gentlemen. . . . France had provided police, judges, gendarmes, prisons, dungeons, and scaffolds for the purpose of fighting illegal

plunder. The law itself conducts this war, and it is my wish and opinion that the law should always maintain this attitude toward plunder. But it does not always do this. Sometimes the law defends plunder and participates in it. Thus the beneficiaries are spared the shame, danger, and scruple which their acts would otherwise involve. Sometimes the law places the whole apparatus of judges, police, prisons, and gendarmes at the service of the plunderers, and treats the victim—when he defends himself—as a criminal. In short, there is a *legal plunder*. . . . But how is this legal plunder to be identified? Quite simply, see if the law takes from some persons what belongs to them, and gives it to other persons to whom it does not belong. See if the law benefits one citizen at the expense of another by doing what the citizen himself cannot do without committing a crime. Then abolish this law without delay, for it is not only an evil itself, but also it is a fertile source for further evils because it invites reprisals. If such a law—which may be an isolated case—is not abolished immediately, it will spread, multiply, and develop into a system. The person who profits from this law will complain bitterly, defending his *acquired rights*. He will claim that the state is obligated to protect and encourage his particular industry; that this procedure enriches the state because the protected industry is thus able to spend more and to pay higher wages to the poor workingmen. Do not listen to this sophistry by vested interests. The acceptance of these arguments will build legal plunder into a whole system.[13]

Government must simply get out of the plunder business and return to its proper role of plunder punisher. Justice for all can only be realized when legalized plunder is eliminated and illegal plunder is promptly punished according to the rule of law.

Distinction

The Five Laws of Decline affect the mental makeup of society's members as well as the physical results by changing the distinctions people seek in society. When the FLD are checked, people seek distinction through "economic means," but if FLD exploitation becomes possible, most people will readily seek "political means" of distinction instead.

Historically, the reward system within society creates the culture, and the culture creates the results. The culture of distinction that society recognizes drives the behavior of its members, which then leads to the results produced. Unfortunately, as discussed in the previous duties, when a society's members resort to "political means" to satisfy wants, a downward slide begins. In short, any society that rewards injustice will experience more injustice. On the other hand, any society that punishes injustice will experience justice for all. Bastiat described this metaphysical shift in society when he wrote about the perversion of law when it rewards exploitation:

> What are the consequences of such a perversion? In the first place, it erases from everyone's conscience the distinction between justice and injustice. No society can exist unless the laws are respected to a certain degree. The safest way to make laws respected is to make them respectable. When law and morality contradict each other, the citizen has the cruel alternative of either losing

> his moral sense or losing his respect for the law. These two evils are of equal consequence, and it would be difficult for a person to choose between them. The nature of law is to maintain justice. This is so much the case that, in the minds of the people, law and justice are one and the same thing. There is in all of us a strong disposition to believe that anything lawful is also legitimate. This belief is so widespread that many persons have erroneously held that things are "just" because law makes them so. Thus, in order to make plunder appear just and sacred to many consciences, it is only necessary for the law to decree and sanction it. Slavery, restrictions, and monopoly find defenders not only among those who profit from them but also among those who suffer from them.[14]

The Bible teaches a similar concept and issues a warning to "those who call evil good and good evil" in Isaiah 5:20 (ESV). However, to keep people believing that evil is good and good is evil requires massive amounts of propaganda from the exploiters. In consequence, any society where the FLD are expanding is also one where the exploiters increasingly take over the media.

Basically, the exploiters seek to control the media to deflect the people's attention from the injustices they are suffering. Instead, by directing their attention to sports and entertainment, stocks and bonds, or contrived political disputes, exploiters keep the people distracted by a drumroll of disinformation and misinformation. The key is to provide them with anything they want except the truth. In effect, the people are lulled to sleep by media either supported or owned by the exploiters themselves.

For instance, Alberto Fujimori, the democratically elected leader of Peru, led a coup that transformed the democracy into a dictatorship in 1992. He relied heavily on the support of his right-hand man, Vladimiro Montesinos, who organized a mass system of bribery, payoffs, and hush money to ensure the support of influential members of Peruvian society for his dictatorship. Revealingly, however, after the fall of Fujimori's government, the meticulously documented records of Montesinos's misdeeds fell into the public's hands. Acemoğlu and Robinson recorded:

> The amounts are revealing about the value of the media to a dictatorship. A Supreme Court judge was worth between $5,000 and $10,000 a month, and politicians in the same or different parties were paid similar amounts. But when it came to newspapers and TV stations, the sums were in the millions. They paid more than $1 million to a mainstream newspaper, and to other newspapers they paid any amount between $3,000 and $8,000 per headline. Fujimori and Montesinos thought that controlling the media was much more important than controlling politicians and judges. One of Montesinos's henchmen, General Bello, summed this up in one of the videos by stating, "If we do not control the television we do not do anything."[15]

Understanding human nature and the FLD, does anyone doubt that similar behavior occurs at some level or another in all societies? True, the influence is less overt and the bribes are rationalized as perks and promotions, but the results are the same. The FLD exploiters use the media to redirect, rationalize, and entertain the people into passivity.

To some extent, every government relies upon the "consent of the governed" in order to continue its rule. Moreover, in a democracy, the media are responsible for the "manufacturing of consent,"[16] as Walter Lippmann observed nearly a century ago. This propaganda model to manufacture consent blossomed as a tool of social control during WWI. The British, realizing they were losing the "war to end all wars" to the Germans, poured millions of pounds into their growing propaganda machine, called the Ministry of Information. The goal was to convince America of the righteousness of the British cause and to help defeat the barbaric "Huns." Noam Chomsky explained:

> The British Ministry documents (a lot have been released) show their goal was, as they put it, to control the thought of the entire world . . . but mainly the US. . . . In the US there was a counterpart. Woodrow Wilson was elected in 1916 on an anti-war platform. . . . But he decided to go to war. So the question was how do you get a pacifist population to become raving anti-German lunatics so they want to go kill all the Germans? That requires propaganda. So they set up the first and really only major state propaganda agency in US history (Committee of Public Information or more commonly called the "Creel Commission" in honor of its founder George Creel). . . . The task of this commission was to propagandize the population into jingoist hysteria. It worked incredibly well. Within a few months the US was able to go to war. . . . [T]he American business community was also very impressed with the propaganda effort. . . . [T]he huge public relations industry, which is a US invention and a monstrous industry, came out of the first World War. . . . Edward Bernays, comes right out of the Creel Commission. He has a book that came out a few years

> afterward called *Propaganda*. . . . The propaganda system of the first World War and this commission that he was part of showed, he says, that it is possible to "regiment the public mind every bit as much as an army regiments their bodies." These new techniques of regimentation of minds, he said, had to be used by "intelligent minorities" in order to make sure that the slobs stay the right course. We can do it now because we have these new techniques.[17]

Presumably, if a few were benefiting from an unjust FLD exploitation over the many, they would focus on building the "consent of the governed" through various propaganda techniques. For only by "manufactured consent" could they continue to enjoy the plunder of society while maintaining a peaceful populace. In fact, after WWI, the big corporations (banks, businesses, and government) hired nearly all the members of the Creel Commission propaganda ministry to improve the public relations of their companies. Naturally, when the companies realized the power of propaganda, they sought not just better messaging but outright ownership of the media outlets to manage the daily messages the masses consumed. The revealing book *The Media Monopoly* explained how big business followed this exact course. When the book first hit US shelves in 1983, author Ben Bagdikian stated, "Fifty corporations dominated almost every mass medium." Significantly, with every new release of the book, the number of corporations controlling the media dropped—from twenty-nine firms in 1987, twenty-three in 1990, and fourteen in 1992 to ten in 1997 and only six today! In other words, six corporations create, print, and deliver the "official" news that the US public consumes.[18]

Indeed, the consolidation of media into a few hands is a dangerous opening for FLD exploitation. For without a free press to act as a watchdog on potential exploitation, more and more daring FLD opportunities will be attempted as the exploiters feel assured that their egregious activities will never see the light of day. Unfortunately, Western society is reaching the point where the plunder is occurring nearly as fast as the propaganda is written to justify it. Noted journalist A. J. Liebling said it best when he remarked, "Freedom of the press is guaranteed to those who own one."[19] This means there are six entities left in America that have freedom of the press.

In reality, however, the six remaining media conglomerates are not truly independent since they are closely connected through interlocking corporate boards. Media critic Mark Crispin Miller connected the dots when he wrote:

> The implications of these mergers for journalism and the arts are enormous. It seems to me that this is, by definition, an undemocratic development. The media system in a democracy should not be inordinately dominated by a few very powerful interests.[20]

But if the goal of the FLD ruling elites is manufacturing consent, then the converging media monopoly is not an accident but the intended result.

Dreams

The last duty of the SDS, the dream duty, is also affected by FLD growth. Every person begins with hope for a better tomorrow, but when the FLD have been activated, State Power coercion increases, and Social Power liberty declines. And with the death of liberty comes the death of dreams. Repeated FLD injustices cause people to stop dreaming because they stop believing hard work can make their dreams come true. Charles Adams explains how FLD excessive taxation attacks the dreams and hopes of the people:

> From the ancients there is much we can learn, especially in the matter of human rights. Liberty came from the Greeks who believed that tyranny was the consequence of the wrong kind of taxation. The Romans made an addendum to the Greek thesis: In any conflict between liberty and taxes, liberty will give ground. . . . When we tax we are dealing with fire, and without proper controls and care, we can easily burn down everything we have built, and our hopes for a better world can go up in smoke. On the other hand, taxes properly controlled have built great nations and brought much good to their inhabitants.[21]

In other words, what point is there in dreaming and sowing if the exploiters are the only ones who reap the increase?

Ridley also explained why the state FLD parasite ends up killing society's SDS host:

> Inventors will not invent unless they can keep at least some of the proceeds of their inventions. After all, somebody will not invest time and effort in planting a crop in his field if he cannot expect to harvest it and keep the profit for himself—a fact Stalin, Mao, and Robert Mugabe learned the hard way.[22]

The state, evidently, never seems to learn this valuable lesson, namely, that people cannot be tamed like animals, for inside of them is a metaphysical urge to dream and grow. Hence, if the state-activated FLD oppress the people, Social Power and the SDS suffer increasing damage until society collapses.

EPILOGUE

Regrettably, few political leaders seem able or willing to apply a systematic mindset to society in general and human nature in specific. Even the few who do tend to view human nature as they want it to be rather than as it truly is. Accordingly, this book has examined Western society's structures to show the productive capacity that results when the Six Duties of Society are free to operate and, by contrast, the destructive capacity of the Five Laws of Decline when they are enabled.

Certainly, understanding the SDS helps society, but that isn't enough. Leaders must also fully comprehend the FLD, or they will inadvertently destroy the society they think they are building. In other words, the unintended consequences society suffers due to ignorance will still destroy it, regardless of whether the leaders are cognizant of this fact. Just as ignorance of gravity doesn't prevent a person from falling when walking off a cliff, ignorance of the FLD doesn't prevent society from failing when their truths are ignored. Leadership in any society must acknowledge and understand both the SDS and FLD, obeying the former and avoiding the latter. Otherwise, as history confirms, destruction is the predictable outcome.

Stories of the rise and fall of civilizations and organizations in history are ubiquitous. A pattern repeats itself again and again:

One generation of leaders obeys the principles of the SDS while restraining the FLD. But then eventually some future generation initiates the FLD while killing the SDS. Therefore, it is crucial to understand that neutralizing the FLD isn't a nice addition to a statesman's toolbox; it is absolutely essential.

Perhaps the best way to truly understand the relevance of the SDS and FLD processes, and to secure their validity in your mind forever, is to examine how their interplay has affected actual historical societies. Indeed, each rise-and-fall cycle experienced by those who have gone before us should display the effects predicted by the interaction of the two processes. This, in fact, is the subject for the next book in this series, *And Justice for All: The Quest for Concord, Volume II: The Problem on Display in History*. In that next volume, we will examine several Greco-Roman (Greek Confederation, Roman Republic, Roman Empire) and Anglo-Saxon (American Confederation, American Republic, and American Empire) societies to see just how the SDS birthed and then the FLD destroyed each one. It is one thing to discuss overall principles, as we have done here in Volume I, but it is quite another to see them actually lived out in the colorful and dramatic panoramas provided by our ancestors. Through such vibrant illustrations as those presented by these various societies, we will clearly identify how each failed in its quest for concord and what lessons for our own time can be gleaned from their attempts.

Because history is relentless and unsentimental, each political structure must pass or fail the test of time. The key to the usefulness of political history is in understanding why some frameworks resisted the FLD, while others did not. Unfortunately, few political leaders allow history to tutor them in these vital truths. Hence, each successive society seems to build its structures upon the same failed foundations as its predecessors did. Evidently, societal leaders would rather repeat past failures than learn from them. Volume II provides six case studies and the important lessons to be learned from each in an effort to rectify these common societal failure modes.

After reviewing numerous and wide-ranging historical societies, the impressive predictive ability of the SDS and FLD models leads to the conclusion that these systematic theories mirror historical truth. Accordingly, all the past failures in the quest for concord can be attributed to societal leaders not comprehending the SDS and FLD. If the whole point of leadership is to rise to challenges, overcome obstacles, and develop plans to win, then every sincere statesman and proponent of freedom today needs to have knowledge of the SDS and the systematic nature of the FLD. Leaders must step into the declining cultural current and make their stand. And the underpinnings of the knowledge of the FLD and the SDS will ensure that such leaders are on solid ground.

NOTES

Foreword

1 Thomas Jefferson to Charles Yancey, 1816, *What Really Happened*, https://whatreallyhappened.com/RANCHO/POLITICS/DOCUMENTS/JEFFERSON/jeff5.html, accessed April 30, 2014.

2 Treye Green, "Words from George Washington: 20 Inspiring Quotes from the First U.S. President," *International Business Times*, February 22, 2014 2:30 PM, copyright 2014 IBT Media Inc., www.ibtimes.com/words-george-washington-20-inspiring-quotes-first-us-president-1557331.

3 "Declaration of Independence: A Transcription," *The Charters of Freedom*, http://www.archives.gov/exhibits/charters/declaration_transcript.html, accessed April 30, 2014.

4 Ibid.

5 George Santayana, *The Life of Reason: Reason in Common Sense* (New York: Charles Scribner's Sons, 1905), 284, Internet Encyclopedia of Philosophy: A Peer-Reviewed Academic Resource, http://www.iep.utm.edu/santayana/.

6 Patrick Henry, in a speech before the Virginia Provincial Convention on March 23, 1775, see George Edward Stanley, *The New Republic 1763-1815*, from the Primary Source History of the United States series (Milwaukee, WI: World Almanac Library, 2005), p. 14.

7 Benjamin Franklin, statement made after the Constitutional Convention in 1787, see Denise McNamara, "How Do You Solve a Problem like Obama?" *RedState*, February 19, 2014 at 02:57 PM, copyright 2014 Town Hall Media, www.redstate.com/diary/denisemcnamara/2014/02/19/solve-problem-like-obama/.

8 James Madison, *Federalist* No. 51, published February 6, 1788, under the pseudonym *Publius*.

Introduction

1 Thomas Hobbes, *Leviathan* (Seven Treasures Publications, 2009).
2 Edmund Opitz, *Religion and Capitalism: Allies, Not Enemies* (New Rochelle, NY: Arlington House, 1970).
3 Murray Rothbard, "Freedom, Inequality, Primitivism, and the Division of Labor" *The Politicization of Society*, edited by Kenneth S. Templeton Jr. (Liberty Fund Inc., 2010).
4 Lord Acton, *Essays on Freedom and Power*, Sixth Printing (Meridian Books, 1962).
5 Opitz, *Religion and Capitalism.*
6 Wilhelm Röpke, *A Humane Economy: The Social Framework of the Free Market* (Wilimington, DE: ISI Books, 1998), p. 91.
7 Rothbard, "Freedom, Inequality, Primitivism, and the Division of Labor."
8 James Madison, *Federalist* No. 51, published February 6, 1788, under the pseudonym *Publius.*
9 Bertrand de Jouvenel, *On Power: Its Nature and the History of Its Growth*, translation by J. F. Huntington (Indianapolis: Liberty Fund, 1993), originally published in Geneva as *Du Pouvoir: Histoire Naturelle de sa Croissance*: Les Éditions Cheval Ailé, 1945.
10 Albert Jay Nock, *Our Enemy, the State*, Large Print Edition (Skyler J. Collins, 2012), pp. 3-4, originally published in 1935.
11 Franz Oppenheimer, *The State* (Black Rose Books, 2007).
12 Margaret Thatcher, interview with Llew Gardner for Thames TV's *This Week* on February 5, 1976, http://www.margaretthatcher.org/speeches/displaydocument.asp?docid=102953.
13 Warren T. Brookes, *The Economy in Mind* (New York: Universe Books, 1982), p. 12.

Chapter One

1 John Locke, *The Second Treatise of Civil Government*, chapter 9, section 123 "Of the Ends of Political Society and Government" (1690), http://oregonstate.edu/instruct/phl302/texts/locke/locke2/2nd-contents.html.
2 Felix Morley, *The Power in the People* (New Brunswick, NJ: Transaction Publishers, 2010), p. 109.
3 Ibid.
4 Claude Frédéric Bastiat, *The Law* (Irvington-on-Hudson, NY: The Foundation for Economic Education, Inc.), http://bastiat.org/en/the_law.html#SECTION_G001.

5 Douglass Cecil North and Robert Paul Thomas, *The Rise of the Western World: A New Economic History* (Cambridge: Cambridge University Press, 1973).
6 Bastiat, *The Law*.
7 Ibid.

Chapter Two

1 Matt Ridley, *The Rational Optimist: How Prosperity Evolves* (New York: Harper Perennial, 2011).
2 William M. Gouge, A Short History of Paper Money and Banking (New York: Augustus M. Kelley Publishers, 1968), http://direct.mises.org/document/3294/A-Short-History-of-Paper-Money-and-Banking.
3 George Reisman, *Capitalism: A Treatise on Economics* (Ottawa, IL: Jameson Books, 1998).
4 Ridley, *The Rational Optimist*.
5 North and Thomas, *The Rise of the Western World*.
6 Ridley, *The Rational Optimist*.
7 Bastiat, *The Law*.
8 Ibid.
9 Jeff Howe, *Crowdsourcing: Why the Power of the Crowd Is Driving the Future of Business* (New York: Crown Business, 2008).
10 Stephen R. Covey, *The 7 Habits of Highly Effective People: Powerful Lessons in Personal Change* (New York: Simon & Schuster, 1989).
11 Ridley, *The Rational Optimist*.
12 Wayne Grudem and Barry Asmus, *The Poverty of Nations: A Sustainable Solution* (Wheaton, IL: Crossway, 2013).
13 Adam Smith, A*n Inquiry into the Nature and Causes of the Wealth of Nations* (Chicago: The University of Chicago Press, 1976), originally published in 1776.
14 Johan Norberg, *In Defense of Global Capitalism* (Washington, DC: Cato Institute, 2003).
15 Bastiat, *The Law*.

Chapter Three

1 Orrin Woodward, *RESOLVED: 13 Resolutions for LIFE* (Flint, MI: Obstaclés Press, 2012).
2 Orrin Woodward and Oliver DeMille, *LeaderShift* (New York: Business Plus Hachette Book Group, 2013).
3 Edmund Burke, *The Portable Edmund Burke*, edited with an introduction by Isaac Kramnick (New York: Penguin Books, 1999).
4 Bastiat, *The Law*.

Chapter Four

1 Theodore Sturgeon, "Sturgeon's Revelation," *Venture Science Fiction Magazine*, March 1958.

2 Benjamin Disraeli, Earl of Beaconsfield, *Lothair* (1870).

3 Chris Brady and Orrin Woodward, *Launching a Leadership Revolution: Mastering the Five Levels of Influence* (Flint, MI: Obstaclés Press, 2012).

4 Jai Singh, "Dell: Apple Should Close Shop," *CNET Business Tech News*, October 6, 1997, 2:00 PM PDT, copyright CBS Interactive Inc., http://news.cnet.com/2100-1001-203937.html.

5 Christopher Bruell, "Xenophon," *History of Political Philosophy*, Third Edition, Edited by Leo Strauss and Joseph Cropsey (The University of Chicago Press, 1987), pp. 99-100.

6 Bastiat, *The Law*.

7 Daron Acemoğlu and James A. Robinson, *Why Nations Fail: The Origins of Power, Prosperity, and Poverty* (New York: Crown Business, 2012), pp. 248-249.

8 Ibid., p. 249.

9 Grudem and Asmus, *The Poverty of Nations*.

10 Margaret Thatcher, February 5, 1976, interview with journalist Llew Gardner on *This Week*, Thames Television Euston Centre, London, copyright Margaret Thatcher Foundation 2014, http://www.margaretthatcher.org/document/102953.

11 Wordvia, The Word Way, definition of *Gresham's Law*, copyright 2013-2014 Wordvia.com, http://www.wordvia.com/dictionary/Gresham%27s%20Law.

12 Jouvenel, *On Power*.

13 Dictionary.com, definition of *Law of Diminishing Returns*, copyright 2014 Dictionary.com, LLC, http://dictionary.reference.com/browse/law+of+diminishing+returns.

14 Ridley, *The Rational Optimist*.

15 Wikipedia, "Newton's Laws of Motion," definition of *Law of Inertia*,Wikimedia Foundation Inc., last modified on April 6, 2011, at 19:51, http://en.wikipedia.org/wiki/User:Totallynuts.

16 Jouvenel, *On Power*.

17 Ibid.

18 Henry Ford, as quoted in "Henry Ford Anniversary Tour Takes a Trip through Industrial Rhineland," *@FordOnline*, June 12, 2013 4:00 AM ET, copyright 2014 Ford Motor Company, http://www.at.ford.com/news/cn/Pages/Henry%20Ford%20Anniversary%20Tour%20Takes%20a%20Trip%20Through%20Industrial%20Rhineland.aspx.

19 Acemoğlu and Robinson, *Why Nations Fail*.

Chapter Five

1 Norberg, *In Defense of Global Capitalism.*
2 Jouvenel, *On Power.*
3 F. A. Hayek, *The Fatal Conceit: The Errors of Socialism,* edited by W. W. Bartley, III (Chicago: University of Chicago Press, 1988).

Chapter Six

1 Ridley, *The Rational Optimist.*
2 Charles-Louis de Secondat, Baron de La Brède et de Montesquieu, *The Spirit of the Laws,* Book 8, chapter 1, translated and edited by Anne M. Cohler, Basia Carolyn Miller, and Harold Samuel Stone (Cambridge University Press, 1989).
3 John Marshall, James McCulloch v. The State of Maryland, John James, 17 U.S. 316 (1819), argued on February 22, 1819, decided on March 6, 1819.
4 Charles Adams, *For Good and Evil: The Impact of Taxes on the Course of Civilization,* second edition (Lanham, MD: Madison Books, 2001).
5 Rothbard, "Freedom, Inequality, Primitivism, and the Division of Labor."
6 Murray N. Rothbard, *The Mystery of Banking,* second edition (Auburn, AL: Ludwig von Mises Institute, 2008).
7 Kevin Dowd, Foreword to *Free Banking: Theory, History, and a Laissez-Faire Model* by Larry J. Sechrest (Auburn, AL: The Ludwig von Mises Institute, 2008).
8 Thomas Jefferson, letter to Thomas Cooper, 1814.
9 Rothbard, *The Mystery of Banking*
10 Ludwig von Mises, *Human Action: A Treatise on Economics* (Auburn, AL: The Ludwig von Mises Institute, 1989).
11 Carl von Clausewitz, *On War* (1832).
12 Bastiat, *The Law.*
13 Ibid.
14 Ibid.
15 Acemoğlu and Robinson, *Why Nations Fail.*
16 Walter Lippmann, *Public Opinion* (New York: Harcourt, Brace and Company, 1922).
17 Noam Chomsky, from a talk at Z Media Institute, June 1997; also appearing in Russ Kick's *You Are Being Lied To: The Disinformation Guide to Media Distortion, Historical Whitewashes and Cultural Myths* (New York: The Disinformation Company Ltd., 2001).
18 Ben Bagdikian, *The Media Monopoly,* fifth edition (Beacon Press, 1997).
19 A. J. Liebling, "Do You Belong in Journalism?," *The New Yorker* (May 14, 1960).

20 Norman Solomon, "Big Media Applaud Big Media Merger," *FAIR Media Beat*, September 9, 1999, http://fair.org/media-beat-column/big-media-applaud-big-media-merger/.
21 Adams, *For Good and Evil.*
22 Ridley, *The Rational Optimist.*

ACKNOWLEDGMENTS

Every book I write seems to follow a similar pattern: it begins with a dream, turns into a nightmare, and finally culminates into the joy of release at its completion. The dream for this book stems from my conviction that increasing State Power is the main cause of the decline of Western civilization. The nightmare occurred when I realized how much additional research was needed in order to do this book the justice it deserved. Indeed, the book stalled for over a year as I studied the role the state plays in the fractional reserve banking system. Thankfully, I am now experiencing the joy associated with the temporary release from my magnificent obsession: *justice for all.* Nonetheless, since this is only the first of a three-part book series, I know the dream-nightmare-release cycle will begin again shortly!

I have been fortunate to be blessed with an amazing wife whose love, encouragement, and patience make my book writing possible. Laurie Woodward is my greatest earthly blessing, and I could not do what I do without her. In fact, not only do my wife and two remaining children living at home, Lance and Jeremy, sacrifice time to allow me to write books, but they are also the first to review them. I want to publicly thank them for reading, commenting, and offering suggestions for improvements on the material entailed in this book.

I would also like to give a special thank you to Chris Brady for going above and beyond the call of duty in editing and re-editing this work. His efforts have ensured that the work is approachable to anyone interested in learning the current challenges facing Western civilization.

In addition, Oliver DeMille, Tim Marks, Claude Hamilton, Bill Lewis, Dan Hawkins, and George Guzzardo have provided a nearly endless stream of encouragement, which was greatly needed in order for me to complete this endeavor.

The talented cast of characters at Obstaclés Press, under the leadership of Rob Hallstrand and including Norm Williams, Michelle Turner, Bill Rousseau, Deborah Brady, and many others, has made the entire publishing process stress-free.

Finally, I would like to thank my Lord and Savior Jesus Christ for saving a ruined sinner desperately in need of His grace. Anything achieved in my life is due to His grace, love, and direction.

OTHER BOOKS BY ORRIN WOODWARD

RESOLVED: 13 Resolutions for LIFE
by Orrin Woodward – $21.95

This book is the perfect way to learn the personal and leadership principles that have made so many people grow from ordinary citizens into extraordinary people who shine. Orrin Woodward takes you back in time to explore the wisdom and experiences of some of the world's most renowned leaders. Also used in college curricula, this book is the ideal gift of "a better you" for yourself and your loved ones. Be *RESOLVED* to develop richer relationships, more personal satisfaction, a compelling sense of purpose, and better control of your finances and business.

Leadership and Liberty: Pieces of the Puzzle
by Chris Brady and Orrin Woodward – $17.95

This is a must read to equip leaders, both new and experienced alike, to make a difference in the fight for freedom. Chris Brady and Orrin Woodward review timeless leadership principles as applied to the concepts of liberty and freedom—specifically toward winning back much of what has been lost in our lands. Get your copy today and start leading the way toward restored freedom!

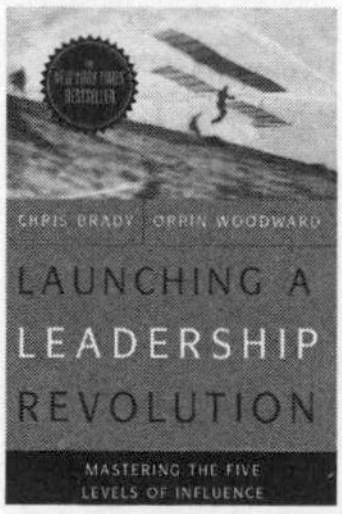

Launching a Leadership Revolution: Mastering the Five Levels of Influence
by Chris Brady and Orrin Woodward – $15.95

This *New York Times* bestseller demonstrates how the principles of leadership apply to anyone and everyone. The question isn't whether you are a leader but, rather, will you be ready when you're called upon to lead? Orrin Woodward and Chris Brady teach you the art and science of leadership, so you *will* be ready when the spotlight shines on you!

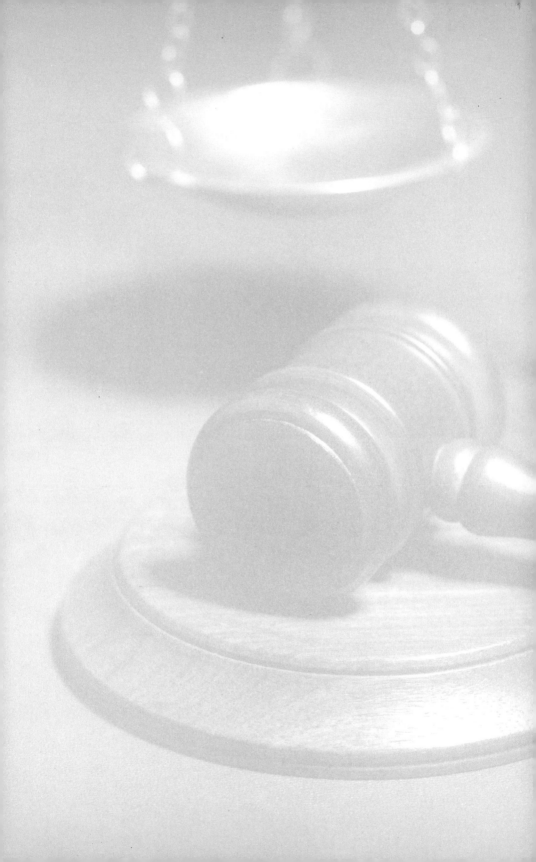